Alicia's Adventuras en Wonderlandia

Alicia's Adventuras en Wonderlandia

Alice's Adventures in Wonderland in Spanglish

Por

Lewis Carroll

ILUSTRACIONES POR
JOHN TENNIEL

TRANSLADADO AL SPANGLISH POR
ILAN STAVANS

evertype

2021

Publicado por/*Published by* Evertype, 19ᴀ Corso Street, Dundee, ᴅᴅ2 1ᴅʀ, Scotland. *www.evertype.com*.

Título original/*Original title*: *Alice's Adventures in Wonderland*.

Esta traducción/*This translation* © 2021 Ilan Stavans.
Esta edición/*This edition* © 2021 Michael Everson.

Ilan Stavans afirma su derecho segun Copyright, Designs and Patents Act 1988, al ser identificado como el traductor de esta obra.
Avner Perez has asserted his right under the Copyright, Designs and Patents Act, 1988, to be identified as the translator of this work.

Primera edición/*First edition* 2021.

Este libro esta registrado en el catálogo del British Library.
A catalogue record for this book is available from the British Library.

ISBN-10 1-78201-252-4
ISBN-13 978-1-78201-252-8

Composición tipográfica en De Vinne Text, Mona Lisa, Engravers' Roman, y Liberty por Michael Everson.
Typeset in De Vinne Text, Mona Lisa, Engravers' Roman, and Liberty by Michael Everson.

Ilustraciones/*Illustrations*: John Tenniel, 1865.

Cubierta/*Cover*: Michael Everson.

Prefacio

La translación nunca es un innocent act: traducir es to interpret; es, also, subvertir.

Esta versión de *Alice's Adventures in Wonderland* en Spanglish es el result de years de trabajo. Empezó, without yo knowing it, cuando yo transladé, in 1999, el first capítulo de Part I de *Don Quixote*. Since then, mi interés en esta hybrid lengua, un back-ad-forth entre el español and English que es neither español o English, se ha incrementado substantially. Spanglish es un global fenómeno that responde a la unavoidable condición del present: la immigración.

It is spoken por approximadamente 50 milliones de personas, no solo en los United States sino en todo el mundo. Un Spanish hablante, en general, es bilingual: español y Spanglish; o English y Spanglish. O even trilingual: español, English y Spanglish. Por qué no darle a esta diasporic nación su propia *Alicia's Adventuras en Wonderlandia*?

Hay una abundancia de border languas today: *franglais, portunhol, hibriya,* etc. Among immigrantes están también las "middle-step" languas: *Yinglish,* por ejemplo, una mixture de Yiddish y English. Spanglish es una border lengua, as well as una "middle-step" lengua. En verdad, no hay un

Spanglish sino una amplia variedad: el Spanglish de los Cuban-Americans, called *Cubonics*; *Dominicanish*, que usan los Dominican-Americans; *Nuyorrican*, de los Puerto Ricans en New York; *Chicano*; y así.

As in otras translaciones mías into Spanglish, mi lectura de la novella de Charles Lutwidge Dodgson, alias Lewis Carroll—which empezó como una story que él, un lecturer de Matemáticas en Christ Church, en July 4th, 1862 (el libro se publicó three years later, en 1865), contó a Alice Liddell, una niña de 10 años, durante un viaje en row-boat por el Thames River en Oxford, in which, además de Alice, were también sus hermanas Lorina Charlotte (known como Elsie) y Edith (Matilda), las tres hijas del dean de Christ Church, y el Rev. Robinson Duckworth—es sobre adderar voces y no subtraerlas.

Spanglish, now en estado de transición de un oral vehicle de communicación a uno written, just como en un punto el español y el English fueron, followea tres estrategias: code switching, syntactic reconfiguración, y el uso de neologismos, en this case llamados Spanglishismos. There are those who dirán que hay otras maneras de transladar Lewis Carroll al Spanglish. Estoy de acuerdo: si hay 22 translaciones de *Don Quixote* al English y 12 de *Crime and Punishment* de Dostoyevsky, por qué no aspirar once again a la pluralidad? What es inquestionable, pa'bien o pa'mal, es que this one es la primera.

Voy a mencionar a few curiosidades, although no todas pa'que el reader no pierda el placer de la sorpresa: I've tried, cuento era pertinente, to keep las rimas de los Lewis Carroll's poems, which en Spanglish might followear los ritmos del English; el caracter de Pat es Irish, pero yo lo he hecho Brazilian; he remplazado las referencias a William the Conqueror con otras a Colón, Isabel La Católica, Torquemada, la Santa Inquisición, el "Ché Guevara, César

Chávez y otros episodios of Hispanic historia; Shakespeare se hace Cervantes y el Cheshire Cat en el Gato de Cheshire; y he llamado a las tres hermanas Elese, Laicia y Tili.

I give gracias a Michael Everson por su invaluable advice.

Ilan Stavans
Amherst, Marzo 2021

Foreword

Translation is never an innocent act: to translate is to interpret; it is, also, to subvert.

This version of *Alice's Adventures in Wonderland* in Spanglish is the result of years of work. It started, without my knowing it, when I translated, in 1999, the first chapter of Part I of *Don Quixote*. Since then, my interest in this hybrid language, a back-ad-forth between Spanish and English that is neither Spanish nor English, has increased substantially. Spanglish is a global phenomenon that responds to an unavoidable condition of the present: immigration.

It is spoken by approximately 50 million people, not only in the United States but in the entire world. A Spanish speaker, in general, is bilingual: Spanish and Spanglish; or English and Spanglish. Or even trilingual: Spanish, English, and Spanglish. Why not give this diasporic nation its own *Alicia's Adventuras en Wonderlandia*?

There is an abundance of border languages today: *franglais, portunhol, hibriya,* etc. Among immigrants there are also "middle-step" languages: *Yinglish,* for instance, a mix of Yiddish and English. Spanglish is a border language, as well as a "middle-step" language. In truth, there is no one Spanglish but an ample variety: the Spanglish of Cuban-Americans, called *Cubonics*; *Dominicanish*, used by Dominican-Americans; *Nuyorrican*, by Puerto Ricans in New York; *Chicano*; and so on.

As in other translations of mine into Spanglish, my reading of the novel by Charles Lutwidge Dodgson, alias Lewis Carroll—which started as a story told by him, a lecturer in Mathematics at Christ Church, on 4 July 1862 (the book was published three years later, in 1865), to Alice Liddell, a 10-year-old girl, during a row-boat trip along the Thames River in Oxford, in which, aside from Alice, were also her sisters Lorina Charlotte (known as Elsie) and Edith (Matilda), the three daughters of the dean of Christ Church, and the Rev. Robinson Duckworth—is about adding voices, not subtracting them.

Spanglish, now in a state of transition from an oral vehicle of communication to a written one, just as at one point Spanish and English were, follows three strategies: code switching, syntactic reconfiguration, and the use of neologisms, in this case called Spanglishisms. There are those who will state that there are other ways to translate Lewis Carroll into Spanglish. I agree: if there are 22 translations of *Don Quixote* into English and 12 of *Crime and Punishment* by Dostoyevsky, why not aspire once again to plurality? What is unquestionable, for better or worse, is that this one is the first.

I will mention a few curiosities, although not all in order not to take away from the reader the pleasure of surprise: I've tried, when pertinent, to keep the rhyme in Lewis Carroll's poems, which in Spanglish might follow the rhythms of English; the character of Pat is Irish, but I have made it Brazilian; I have replaced the references to William the Conqueror with others to Columbus, Queen Isabella,

Torquemada, the Holy Office, "Ché" Guevara, Cesar Chavez, and other episodes in Hispanic history; Shakespeare becomes Cervantes and the Cheshire Cat in el Gato de Cheshire; and I have called the three sisters Elese, Laicia, y Tili.
I thank Michael Everson for his invaluable advice.

Ilan Stavans
Amherst, March 2021

Prefacio

La traducción nunca es un acto inocente: traducir es interpretar; es, también, subvertir.

Esta versión de *Alice's Adventures in Wonderland* en Spanglish es el resultado de años de trabajo. Empezó, sin yo saberlo, cuando traduje, en 1999, el primer capítulo de la Primera Parte de *Don Quijote*. Desde entonces, mi interés en esta lengua híbrida, un ir y venir entre el español y el inglés que ni es español ni inglés, ha incrementado enormemente. El Spanglish es un fenómeno mundial que responde a esa condición inobjetable del presente: la inmigración.

Lo hablan hoy unos 50 millones de personas, no únicamente en Estados Unidos sino en todo el mundo. El Spanglish-parlante, por lo general, es bilingüe: español y Spanglish; o inglés y Spanglish. Puede, asimismo, ser trilingüe: español, inglés y Spanglish. ¿Por qué no darle a esta nación diaspórica su propia *Alicia's Adventuras en Wonderlandia*?

Hay un sinnúmero de lenguas fronterizas hoy: *franglais*, *portunhol*, *hibriya*, etc. Entre inmigrantes además hay lenguas intermedias: *Yinglish*, por ejemplo, una mezcla de idish e inglés. El Spanglish es una lengua fronteriza, así como una lengua intermedia. En realidad, no hay un Spanglish sino una amplia variandad: el Spanglish de los cubanoamericanos, llamado *Cubonics*; el *Dominicanish* de los dominicano-americanos; el *Nuyorrican* de los puertorriqueños en Nueva York; el *Chicano*; y demás.

Como en otras traducciones mías al Spanglish, mi aproximación a la novela de Charles Lutwidge Dodgson, alias Lewis Carroll—que empezó como un cuento que él, que entonces ensenaba matemáticas en Christ Church, contó el 4 de julio de 1862 (el libro se publicó tres años después, en 1865) a Alice Liddell, una niña de 10 años, durante una travesía en lancha de remos por el Río Támesis de Oxford, en el que, además de Alice, iban las hermanas Lorina Charlotte (también llamada Elsie) y Edith (Matilda), las tres hijas del decano de Christ Church, y el Rev. Robinson Duckworth—es la de sumar voces en vez de restarlas.

El Spanglish, ahora en un estado transición de un vehículo de comunicación oral a uno escrito, como en su momento lo estuvieron el inglés y el castellano, sigue tres estrategias: el cambio de códigos, la reconfiguración sintáctica, y el uso de neologismos, llamados en este caso Spanglishishismos. Por supuesto, habrá quien asegure que hay otras maneras de traducir al Spanglish a Lewis Carroll. Estoy de acuerdo: si hay 22 traducciones del *Quijote* al inglés y 12 de *Crimen y castigo* de Dostoievski, ¿por qué no aspirar otra vez a la pluralidad? Lo que es incuestionable es que, para bien o para mal, esta es la primera.

Menciono algunas curiosidades, aunque no todas para no privar al lector del placer de la sorpresa: he intentado mantener, cuando es deseable, la rima de los poemas de Lewis Carroll, que en Spanglish pueden seguir el ritmo del inglés; el personaje de Pat es irlandés, pero yo lo he reconfigurado como brasileño; he reemplazado las referencias a William de Conqueror con otras a Colón, Isabel La Católica, Torquemada, el Santo Oficio, el Ché Guevara,

César Chávez y otros episodios en la historia hispánica; Shakespeare se convierte en Cervantes y el Cheshire Cat en el Gato de Cheshire; y he llamado a las tres hermanas Elese, Laicia y Tili.

Agradezco a Michael Everson por su invaluable consejo.

Ilan Stavans
Amherst, Marzo 2021

Alicia's Adventuras en Wonderlandia

Contenido

I. Down el Rabit-Hoyo 7

II. La Pool de Lágrimas 16

III. Un Caucus-carrera
y una Long Cola 25

IV. El Rabit Manda una Pequeña Bill 33

V. Consejo del Caterpilar 44

VI. Pig y Peper 56

VII. Un Tea-Party de Locos 68

VIII. El Croque-Piso de la Reina 78

IX. La Story de la Mock Tortuga 89

X. La Cuadrilla del Lobster 99

XI. Quién se Robó las Tartas? 109

XII. Alicia's Evidencia 117

Todos en la golden afternoon
    Muy leisurely we glide;
Por ambos nuestros oars, con mini skill,
    Por little bracitos are plied,
As little manitas hacen vain pretence
    Nuestros wanderings pa'guide.

Ah, cruel Three! En such una hour,
    Bajo tan dreamy weather,
Pa'pedir un cuento of breath tan weak
    Pa'stir la tiniest feather!
Yet qué can una poor voz avail
    Against tres lenguas together?

Imperious Prima flashea forth
    Su edicto "pa'begin it':
En gentler tonos Secunda hopes
    'No habrá tonterías in it!'
While Tertia interrupe el tale
    No más que once un minute.

Anon, pal'sudden silencio won,
    En fancy they pursue
El dream-child moviendo through una landia
    De wonders wild y new,
En friendly chateo con pájaro o beast—
    Y medio believe es true.

Y ever, as el cuento drained
   Los pozos de fancy dry,
Y faintly strovea ese weary one
   Pa'poner el sujeto by,
"El rest next tiempo—" "Es el next time!"
   Las happy voces cry.

Así creció el cuento de Wonderlandia:
   Así slowly, one to one,
Sus quaint eventos eran hammereados out—
   Y now el cuento es done,
Y a casa steereamos, una merry crew,
   Debajo del setting sun.

Alice! Un niñoso cuento take,
   Y, con una gentle hand,
Ponlo donde la Niñez's sueños entwined
   En Memoria's mystic band,
Como peregrino's wither'd wreath de flowers
   Pluqueada en una far-off *landia*.

Down el Rabit-Hoyo

Alicia was beginning to estar muy tireada of sentarse by su hermana on the banco, and of having nada que hacer: once or dos veces she had peepeado into el libro que su hermana was leyendo, pero it had no pincturas o conversationes in it, "pa'qué sirve un libro," pensó Alicia "sin pincturas o conversationes?"

So ella estaba considerando in her propia mente (lo major que she could, porque el hot día made her sentirse muy sleepy and estúpida), whether el placer de making una daisy-cadena iba a ser worth el trouble de getting pa'rriba y picking las daisies, when de repente un rabit blanco con pink ojos ran cerca de ella.

There was nada so *muy* remarcable en eso; ni Alicia pensó it so *very* mucho out of the camino to oir al rabit decir to sí mismo, "Órale dear! Órale dear! Voy a'star late!" (cuando ella pensó it otra vez afterwards, it occurrió a ella que ella ought to have wondereando at esto, pero en este tiempo it all seemed super natural); pero when el rabit actuamente took un reloj out de su waistcoat-bolsillo, and looked at it, and

luego hurried on, Alicia empezó to her feet, porque it flashed
en medio de su mind que she had nunca antes seen un rabit
con either un waistcoat-bolsillo, or a reloj to take out de él,
and burning con curiosidad, she ran en medio del the field
after él, and afortunadamente was just a tiempo to see it pop
down un large rabit-hoyo debajo del hedge.

En another momento down fue Alicia after él, nunca once
considereando how en el mundo she was to get afuera otra
vez.

El rabit-hoyo fue straight on como un tunel por some way,
y entonced dippeó sudenmente abajo, so sudenmente que
Alicia had no un momento pa'pensar about stopping herself
antes de foundearse a sí misma cayendo down un muy deep
pozo.

Either el pozo era muy deep, o ella cayó muy slowly, porque ella had plenty de tiempo as she went down pa'ver about her and pa'wonderear qué was going to pasar next. Primero, ella tried de look abajo and make out dónde ella was coming hacia, pero it was too oscuro to see nada; luego she looked a los sides del pozo, y noticeó que ellos estaban filled con cupboards y book-shelves; aquí y allá ella vio mapas y picturas hung de pegs. Ella took down el jar from de uno de los shelves mientras pasaba; estaba labeleado "ORANGE MARMELADA", pero to her gran disappointment it was vacío: ella no quería dropear el jar por fear de killing a alguien, so ella manageó to ponerlo into uno de los cupboards miesntras she fell past él.

"Caramba!" pensó Alicia pa'sí misma, "after tanto fall as this, yo voy a pensar nothing de tumbling down las escaleras! How bravo they'll all piensan de mi en la casa! Why, yo wouldn't say nada about it, even if I fell off el top de la the casa!" (Which was muy likely verdad.)

Pa'bajo, pa'bajo, pa'bajo. Would la caída *nunca* come to un final! "I wonder cuántas millas I've fallen en este tiempo?" ella dijo aloud. "Yo must estar getting somewhere cerca del centro of la tierra. Let me ver: eso sería cuatro thousand millas down, yo creo—" (for, tu sabes, Alicia había aprendido several cosas of this tipo in her lecciones en la escuela, y though esto was not a *muy* buena oportunidad pa'showing off su knowledge, as there había no one pa'listen to ella, still era good práctica to say it over) "—yes, eso es about la right distancia—pero then yo wondereo que Latitud o Longitud yo tengo to go to?" (Alicia no tenía idea what Latitud era, o Longitud tampoco, pero pensó que erannice grand palabras pa'decir.)

Presentemente ella empezó otra vez. "I wonder si yo shall caer right *through* la tierra! Qué funny it'll seem to salir among la gente que camina with sus cabezas downward! Las antipatías, yo creo—" (ella estaba algo contenta there *was* nadie listeneando, este tiempo, as it didn't sonar at all como la right palabra) "—pero I shall tener que preguntarles what el nombre de su country es, tú sabes. Por favor, Ma'am, esta es New Zealandia o Australia?" (y ella trató to curtsear as she habló—fancy *curtseando* as you're cayendo through el aire! Do you think tú podrías could managearlo?) "Y qué ignorante little niñita she'll pensar que soy for preguntar! No, it'll never do to preguntar: quizás I shall verlo escrito somewhere."

Pa'bajo, pa'bajo, pa'bajo. There was nada más que hacer, so Alicia soon empezó a hablar otra vez. "Dinah ne va a extrañar very mucho esta noche, I should pensar!" (Dinah was el gato.) "Espero que se acuerden de su saucer de leche en el tea-tiempo. Dinah my dear! I wish you were aquí abajo with me! No hay ratones en el aire, I'm afraid, pero tu puedes catchar un bat, and that's muy like un ratón, tú sabe. Pero do gatos comen bats, yo wondereo?" And aquí Alicia began to sentirse muy sleepy, y went on diciendo to ella misma, en un dreamy sort of way, "Do gatos comen bats? Do gatos comen bats?" y sometimes, "Do bats comen gatos?" for, tú ves, as ella couldn't answerear either cuestión, no importaba mucho which way ella lo ponía. Ella felteaba that ella se estaba dozing off, y had just begun to soñar que ella estaba walkeando mano a mano con Dinah, y saying al gato muy earnestly, "Pus, Dinah, tell me la verdá: did you comer un bat?" cuando suddenly, thump! thump! Abajo cayó ella en un heap de sticks and dry hojas, y la fall estaba over.

Alicia estaba un poco hurt, y ella jumpeó up on to sus pies en un momento: ella lukeó up, pero todo estaba dark encima de su cabeza; before ella estaba otro long pasaje, and el rabit blanco estaba still en sight, hurreando down. No había un momento to be lost: away fue Alicia like el viento, y estaba just a tiempo pa'oir it say, mientras turneaba la corner, "Oh mis erejas y mis whiskers, how tarde it's getting!" Ella estaba cerca behind it cuando ell turneó la corner, pero el rabit was no longer pa'ser visto: ella se foundeó en un long, low hall, que estaba lit up por un row de lámparas hanging del rufo.

Había puertas all round el hall, pero estaban todas lockeadas; y cuando Alicia había estado all the way abajo one side y up el otro side, tratando every puerta, ella walkeó tristemente down el medio, wondereando cómo ella iba to get out otra vez.

Suddenly ella came upon una little tres-legged mesita toda hecha de solid vidrio; no había nada on it except una tiny golden llave, and Alicia's first pensamiento fue que it might pertenecer to una de las puertas del hall; pero, alas! either los locks eran demasiado grandes, o la llave era demasiado small, pero at any rate no podía abrir any de ellas. Sin embargo, en el segundo tiempo around, ella came upon a low cortina que ella no había noticed antes, y behind ella estaba una little puertita de about quince inches high: ella trató la little golden llavecita en el locy para su gran delight fitteaba!

Alicia abrió la puerta y foundeó que ella ledeaba a un small pasaje, no más grande que un rat-hoyo: ella se knelteó hacia abajoy lookeó along el pasaje into el loveliest jardín you ever visto. Cuánto ella longed to salir del dark hall, y wanderear about entre esas camas de bright flores y esas cool fuentes, pero ella ni squiera pudo get her cabeza through la doorway; "y even si mi cabeza would go through," pensó la pobre Alicia, "it would be de muy poco uso without mis hombros. Oh, cómo yo wisheo que yo pudiera shut up como un telescopio! Yo creo que yo podría, if I only saber cómo empezar." For, tú sabes, so muchas out-of-the-way cosas had happened lately, que Alicia had empezar to pensar que very few cosas de verdá eran súper imposibles.

There seemed to haber no uso en waitear en la little puertita, so ella went de regreso a la mesa, halfesperando que ella might findear otra llave on ella, o en any rate un libro de reglas pa'shuttear gente up como telescopios: esta vez ella foundeó una little botellita sobre ella, ("que certainly no estaba allí before," dijo Alicia,) y round el neck de la botella estaba un label de papel, con las palabras "DRINQUÉAME" beautifulmente printeadas en ella en large letras.

Estaba muy very bien to decir "Drinquéame", pero la wise little Alicia no iba a hacer *that* en un hurry. "No, I'll lookear primero," ella dijo, "y ver whether está markada *'poison'* o no"; porque ella había leído several nice little historias sobre niños who had got quemados, y eaten up por wild bestias y otras unpleasant cosas, todo because ellos *would* no remembrear la simple regla que sus amigos had taught a ellos: such como, que un red-caliente poker te puede burn you si tu holds it too cerca; y que if you te cortas tu dedo *muy* deeply con un cuchillo, usualmente bleedey ella nunca había forgeteado eso,

que, si tu drinkeas mucho de una botella markada "poison",
es casi certain to disagreder contigo, sooner o later.

Pero, esta botella *no* estaba markeada "poison", so Alicia
ventureó a tastearla, y findeando que estaba muy nice,
(tenía, in facto, una sort de flavors mixteados de cherry-
tarta, custardo, pine-manzana, roast pavo, toffee, y tostado
caliente con mantequilla,) ella muy soon lo finisheó.

"Qué feeling más curioso!" dijo Alicia; "Yo debo estar
shutteando up como un telescopio."

Y so así era: ella tenía now solo diez inches high, y su cara
brightened pa'rriba en el thought que ella tenía ahora el right

size pa'going through la little puertita into ese lovely jardín. Primero, however, ella waiteó por unos minutos pa'ver si ella was going to shrinkear más: ella se sintió un poquito nerviosa sobre esto; "for it might terminar, tú sabes," dijo Alicia to ella misma, "en mi going afuera altogether, como una candle. I wonder quién voy a ser entonces?" Y ella trató to fancear what la flama de la candle es cómo después de que ls candle está blowneada, porque ella no podía remembrear ever having visto such cosa.

After un rato, findeando que nada más was happening, ella decidió ir al jardín at once; pero, alas pa'la pobre Alicia! Cuando ella got a la puerta, ella foundeó que ella had forgotteneado la little golden llavecita, y cuando ella wentde regreso a la mesa for ella, ella foundeó que ella could not posiblemente reachearla: ella could watchearla muy plenamente through el vidrio, y ella trató su best pa'climbear una de las piernas de la mesa, pero estaba too slippery; y cuando ella had cansado herself out de tratar, la pobre little cosita se sentó down y lloró.

"Pucha, there's no uso de llorar like that!" dijo Alicia pa'sí misma, algo sharpeamente; "yo te adviseo que tu leave off en este minuto!" Ella generalmente gave pa'sí misma very good consejo, (though ella muy seldom lo followeaba), y sometimes ella escoldeaba a sí misma tan severamente as to traer lágrimas into sus ojos; y once ella remembereaba trying to boxear sus own eídos por having cheateado a sí misma en un juego de croqueta ella estaba jugando against ella misma, pues esta curious niña era muy fond de pretender serdos personas. "Pero it is no uso ahora," pensó la pobre Alicia, "to pretender ser dos personas! Why, there's hardly suficiente de mí pa'cer *una* respectable persona!"

Soon su ojo cayó en una little glass cajita que estaba lying under la mesa: ella la abrió, and found adentro un muy small pastel, on which las palabras "CÓMEME" estaban beautifully marcadas con currantes. "Pus, me lo voy a comer," dijo Alicia, "and if me hace crecer más grande, yo puedo reachear la llave; and if me hace crecer más chica, yo puedo creepear under la puerta; so either way yo voy a llega al jardín, y me vale which happens!"

Ella comió un little poquito, y dijo anxiosamente a ella misma, "Which camino? Which camino?", holdeando su mano en la top de su cabeza pa'sentir which dirección estaba growing, y ella estaba muy sorprendida de findear que ella remained la misma size: to be segura, esto generalmente happens cuando uno come pastel, pero Alicia had got tanto into el way de expectear nada pero out-of-the-way cosas to pasar, que it seemed muy dull y estúpido for la vida to continuar en el way común.

So ella set to trabajar, and muy soon finisheó off el pastel.

*   *   *   *

*   *   *

*   *   *   *

CAPÍTULO II

La Pool de Lágrimas

"*C*uriouso and curiouso!" gritó Alicia (she estaba tan surprised, que for el momento she quite forgoteó como hablar buen English); "now me estoy abriendo like el largest telescopio que ever existió! Good-bye, pies!" (porque when she miró down at sus pies, ellos seemed to estar casi fuera de sight, se estaban llendo tan far off). "Oh, mis pobres little piecitos, I wondereo quién will ponerte tus shoes y stocketes now, dears? Estoy segura *I* sha'n't be capaz! Voy a estar a great deal muy far off para troublearme myself sobre ti: tú must managear the best way que puedas—pero yo necesito ser kind a ellos," pensó Alicia, "or perhaps no van a walkear the way yo quiero que caminen! Let me ver: les voy a dar un nuevo pair de bootas every Navidad."

Y siguió planneando para herself cómo she would managear it. "Ellos must ir por el carrier," she pensó; "y how funny it'll parecer, sending presentes a one's own pies! Y qué odd las directiones will lookear!

Alice's Pie Derecho, Esq.,
Hearthrug,
cerca del Fender,
(con Alicia's amor).

Oh dear, qué tonterías estoy talkeando!"

Just entonces her cabeza struqueó against el roofo del hall: in facto ella estaba now más de nueve feet alta, y ella at once toqueó up la little golden llavecita y hurriedó off a la puerta del jardín.

Pobre Alicia! Era lo máximo que ella could hacer, lying abajo on one lado, to ver through into el jardín con un ojo; pero para pasar through was más hopeless que nunca: ella se sateó down y empezó a llorar again.

"You ought to estar avergonzada of yourself," dijo Alicia, "a great niña like you," (she might bien say this), "to go on crying in this way! Stop this momento, I tell you!" Pero she went on all the same, shedding gallons of tears, until there was una gran pool all round ella, unas cuatro inches deep y reacheando half down el hall.

After un tiempo she heard a little pattering of pies en la distancia, y ella hastily secó her ojos pa'ver what was coming. Era el Rabit Blanco returneando, splendidamente vestido, with a pair of white kid guantes en una mano y un large fan en la otra: he came trotting along in a great hurry, muttering to himself as he came, "Oh! La Duquesa, la Duquesa! Oh! wo'n't she be salvaje if I've kept her esperando!" Alicia felt so desesperada que ella estaba ready pa'pedir ayuda de any one; so, when el Rabit came near her, she began, en una low, timid voz, "If you puede, sir—" El Rabit started violentamente, droppeó los white kid guantes y el fan, y skurrieó away into the darkness as duro as he could go.

Alicia took up el fan y guantes, y, as the hall was muy caliente, she kept fanneando herself all the tiempo she seguía talking: "Dear, dear! How extraño todo is to-day! Y yesterday las cosas went on just as usual. I wonder if I've been cambiando en la noche? Let me pensar: was I the same when I got up this morning? I casi pienso I can remembrear sentirme un little diferente. Pero if I'm not the same, la next cuestión es, Who in the world am I? Ah, *that's* the great puzzle!" Y ella empezó thinking over all the niños she knew que were of la same edad as herself, pa'ver if she could have been cambiando for any of them.

"I'm sure I'm not Ada," ella dijo, "for her pelo goes in such long ringlets, y mine doesn't go in ringlets at all; y I'm sure I can't be Mabel, for I know all sorts of cosas, y ella, oh! she knows such very little! Besides, *she's* she, y I'm I, y—oh dear, how puzzling it all is! I'll try if I know all the cosas I used to saber. Let me see: four times five is twelve, y four times six is thirteen, y four times seven is—oh dear! I shall never get to veinte at that rate! Pero, the Multiplicación Table doesn't signify: let's try Geografía. London is the capital of Paris, y Paris es la capital de Roma, y Roma—no, *that's* all wrong, I'm segura! I must have been cambianda for Mabel! I'll try y say '*How doth the little*—'" y ella crosseó her hands on her lap as if she were saying lecciones, y began to repetir it, pero su voz sounded hoarse y extraña, y las palabras did not come the same as they used to do:—

> *"Qué doth el little crocodile*
> *Improve su shining tail,*
> *And pour las aguas of el Nile*
> *En every golden scale!*

"Qué cheerfully he seems to grin,
Cuán neatly spread sus claws,
And welcome little peces in
Con gently sonriente jaws!"

"I'm sure those are not las right palabras," dijo la pobre Alicia, y sus ojos filled with tears ora vez as she went on, "I must be Mabel después de todo, y I shall have to go y live en esa poky little casita, y have next to no toys pa'jugar con, y oh! ever so many lecciones pa'prender! No, I've made up my mind about it; if I'm Mabel, I'll stay down here! It'll be no use their putting sus cabezas down y saying 'Come up otra vez, dear!' I shall only look up y say 'Who am I then? Tell me that first, y then, if I like being that person, I'll come up: if not, I'll stay down here till I'm somebody else'—pero, oh dear!" cried Alicia, with a sudden burst of tears, "I do wish they *would* put sus cabezas down! I am so *very* tired of being all alone here!"

As ella dijo esto she looked down a sus manos, y was surprised de ver that she had put on one of el Rabit's little white kid guantes mientras ella hablaba. "How *can* I have done that?" ella pensó. "I must be growing pequeña otra vez." She got up y went to the table pa'medir herself by it, y found that, as nearly as she could guess, she was now about two feet high, y seguía shrinquenado rapidamente: she soon found out that the cause of this was el fan she was holding, y ella lo droppeó hastily, just a tiempo to avoid shrinqueando away altogether.

"That *was* un narrow escape!" dijo Alicia, a good deal frightened at the sudden cambio, pero very contenta de encontrar herself still in existence; "y now for el jardín!" y ella ran with all speed back to la little puertita: pero, alas! la little puertecita was shut otra vez, y la little golden llavecita was lying on the glass table as before, "y las cosas are worse than ever," pensó la pobre child, "for I never was so small as this before, never! Y I declare it's too bad, that it is!"

As ella dijo estas palabras her foot slipped, y in another momento, splash! she was hasta su barbilla de salt water. Her first idea was that she had somehow fallen into the sea, "y in that case I can go de regreso by railway," ella dijo pa'sí misma. (Alicia había estado en el seaside una vez en su vida, y had come a la conclusión general, that wherever you go to on the English coast you find a number of bathing machines in the sea, some niños digging en la sand with spade de maderas, then a row of lodging casas, y behind them una estación de railway.) Pero, she soon made out that she was en un pool de lágrimas which ella had wept when ella era nine feet high.

"I wish I hadn't cried so mucho!" dijo Alicia, as she swam about, trying to find her way out. "I shall be punished for it now, I suppose, by being drowned in my own tears! That *will* be una cosa extraña, to be sure! Pero, todo es extraño hoy."

Just then ella escuchó algo splashing about en la pool un poquito way off, y ella swam nearer pa'saber what it was: at first ella pensó it must be a walrus or hipopótamo, y luego ella remembreó how small she was now, y ella soon made out que era solo un ratón that had slipped in like herself.

"Would it be of any use, now," pensó Alicia, " pa'hablar con este ratón? Todo está so out-of-the-way down here, that I should pensar very likely it can talk: at any rate, there's no harm in trying." So she began: "O Ratón, sabes tú the way out de esta pool? I am muy tired of swimming about here, O Ratón!" (Alicia pensó esta must ser la right manera of speaking to a ratón: she had never done such a cosa before, pero ella remembreó haber visto en su brother's Latin Grammar, "Un ratón—de un ratón—a un ratón—un ratón—O ratón!" El ratón lookeó at her algo inquisitively, y le parecía a ella to winquear con uno de sus little ojitos, pero dijo nada.

"Perhaps it doesn't understand English," pensó Alicia; "I daresay it's un ratón francés, come over con Colón el Descubridor." (For, with all her knowledge of history, Alicia tenía no very clear una noción de how long ago anything había pasado o no.) So ella began otra vez: "Où est ma chatte?" which era la primera sentence de su French lección-book. El Ratón gave un sudden leap fuera del agua, y seemed to quivear todo el rato with fright. "Oh, I beg your pardon!" cried Alicia hastily, afraid that she had hurt el pobre animalito's feelings. "I quite forgotié que no te gustan los gatos."

"Not like gatos!" gritó el Ratón, en una voz shrill, apasionada. "Would *you* like gatos if you were me?"

"Bien, quizás not," dijo Alicia in a soothing tono: "don't be angry about it. Y yet I wish I could show you our gato Dinah: yo pienso you'd take a fancy to los gatos if you could only see her. She is such a dear quiet cosa," Alicia siguió, half pa'sí misma, as she swam lazily about en la pool, "y ella sits purring so nicely by the fire, liqueando her paws y lavando su cara—y ella is such a nice soft cosa pa'nursear—y she's such a capital one for catching ratones—oh, I beg your pardon!" cried Alicia otra vez, for esta vez el Ratón estaba bristleando all over, y ella felt segura it must estar súper offended. "We wo'n't talk about her any more if you'd preferir not."

"We indeed!" gritó el Ratón, who was trembling down to the end of his tail. "As if I would talk on such a sujeto! Our family always *hated* gatos: nasty, low, vulgar cosas! Don't let me hear el nombre otra vez!"

"I wo'n't indeed!" dijo Alicia, in a great hurry to cambiar el sujecto de conversación. "Are you—are you fond—of—of perros?" El ratón no contestó, so Alicia went on eagerly: "Hay un such a nice little perrito near our casa I should like pa'mostrarte! A little bright-eyed terrier, tú sabes, with oh, such long curly brown pelo! Y it'll fetch cosas when you throw them, y it'll sit up y beg for its dinner, y all sorts of cosas— yo no puedo remembrear half of them—y it belongs to a farmer, tú sabes, y he says it's so useful, it's worth a hundred pounds! He says it kills all the rats y—oh dear!" cried Alicia in a sorrowful tono, "Me temo que I've offended it otra vez!" For el Ratón estaba swimmeando away from her as hard as it could go, y making quite una commoción en la pool as it went.

So she called softly after it, "Querido Ratón! Do come back otra vez, y we wo'n't talk about gatos o perros either, if you don't like them!" Cuando el ratón oyó esto, it turned round y swam slowly back to her: su cara estaba muy pale (con pasión, Alicia pensó), y dijo en una low trembleante voz, "Let us get a la shore, y then I'll tell you mi historia, y you'll understand por qué it is I hate gatos y perros."

It was high tiempo pa'irse, for la pool was getting quite crowded with los pájaros y animales que had fallen into it: there were un Duck y un Dodo, un Lory y un Eaglet, y algunas otras curious creaturas. Alicia led el camino, y todo el grupo swameó a la shore.

Un Caucus-carrera y una Long Cola

They eran indeed un extraña-looking gruppo that assembled en el bank—los pájaros with draggled plumas, los animales con su fur clinging close a ellos, y all drippeando mojados, cross, y uncomfortables.

La first cuestión of course era, how to get dry otra vez: they had a consultación about this, y after unos minutos it seemed quite natural to Alicia to find herself hablando familiarly with them, as if she had known them toda su vida. Indeed, she had quite a long argumento with el Lory, who at last turned sulky, y would only say, "I am older than you, y must know better"; y this Alicia would not allow without knowing how old it was, y, as el Lory positively refuseó to tell su edad, there was nada más que decir.

At last el Ratón, who seemed to be una persona of authority among them, called out, "Sit down, todos ustedes, y listen a mí! *I'll* soon make you dry enough!" They all sat down a la vez, in a large ring, con el Ratón en medio. Alicia kept sus

ojos anciosamente fixed on it, for ella se sintió segura she
would catch a bad cold if she did not get dry muy soon.

"Ahem!" dijo el Ratón with an important air, "are you all
ready? Esta es the driest cosa I know. Silence all round, if
you puede! 'Colón, el Descubridor, whose cause was favoured
by Isabella La Católica, was soon la submitteó a la Corona,
que necesitaba marineros, y recientemente había estado
acostumbrada a la usurpación y la conquista. Pedro de
Arbúes y Tomás de Torquemada, inquistors of the Santo
Oficio de la Inquisición—'"

"Ugh!" dijo el Lory, con un shiver.

"I beg your perdón!" dijo el Ratón, frowning, pero muy
politely: "Did you speak?"

"No yo!" dijo el Lory hasteamente.

"I thought you did," dijo el Ratón. "—Yo procedo. 'Ché
Guevara y Alberto Granado, durante su viaje on motorcycle,
declararon for él: y even César Chávez, el activista de los
Farm Workers del American Southwest, found it
advisable—'"

"Found *what?*" dijo el Pato.

"Found *it*," el ratón replicó algo crossly: "of course tú sabes what 'it' means."

"I know what 'it' means bien enough, when I find a cosa," dijo el Pato: "it's generally a frog or a worm. La cuestión es, what did the activista find?"

El ratón no noticeó esta cuestión, pero hurriedly went on, "'—found it advisable to go with Tomás de Torquemada to meet Colón y ofrecerle una dispensación in order not to be persecuted as un converso. Colón's conducta at first era moderada. Pero la insolencia de sus súbditos—' Cómo are you getting on now, my dear?" it continued, turning to Alicia mientras hablaba.

"As wet como siempre," dijo Alicia in a melancholy tono: "it doesn't seem to dry me at all."

"In that case," dijo el Dodo solemnemente, riseando to its feet, "I move that the meeting adjourn, for the immediate adopción of more energetic remedies—"

"Speak Inglés!" dijo la Eaglet. "I don't know the meaning of half those long words, y, what's more, I don't believe you do either!" Y the Eaglet bent down its cabeza to hide a smile: some of los otros pájaros tittered audiblemente.

"What I was going to decir," dijo el Dodo en un tono offendido, "was, that the best cosa to get us dry would be a Caucus-race."

"What *is* a Caucus-race?" dijo Alicia; not that she wanted mucho to know, pero el Dodo had paused as if it thought that *somebody* ought to speak, y no one else seemed inclined to say algo.

"Why," dijo el Dodo, "the best way to explain it is to do it." (Y, as you might like to try la cosa yourself, some winter día, I will tell you how el Dodo managed it.)

Primero it marked out a race-course, in a sort of círculo, ("the exact shape doesn't matter," decía,) y luego all the grupo were placed along the course, here y there. There was no "One, two, three, y away," pero they began running when they liked, y left off donde they gustaron, so that no era fácil to know cuándo la race was terminada. Pero, when ellos habían estado running media hora or so, y were quite dry otra vez, el Dodo suddenly called out "La race ya terminó!" y ellos all crowdeearon round it, panteando, y preguntando, "Pero quién has won?"

Esta cuestión el Dodo could not responder without un gran deal of pensamiento, y it sat for a long tiempo with un dedo pressed upon its forehead (la posición in which you usually see Cervantes, en las pinturas de él), while the rest waited in silence. At last el Dodo dijo, "*Everybody* has won, y all must have premios."

"Pero who is to give los premios?" quite un coro de voces preguntó.

"Why, *ella* of course," dijo el Dodo, pointing a Alicia con un dedo; y all the grupo at once crowded round her, calling out in a confused way, "Premios! Premios!"

Alicia had no idea what to do, y in despair she put su mano in her pocket, y pulled out a box of comfits, (luckily the salt water had not got into it), y handed them round as premios. There was exactly one a-pieza all round.

"Pero she must have un premio herself, tú sabes," dijo el Ratón.

"Of course," el Dodo replicó muy gravely. "What else have you got en tu pocket?" él siguió, turning a Alicia.

"Only a thimble," dijo Alicia tristemente.

"Hand it over here," dijo el Dodo.

Then they all crowded round ella una vez más, while the Dodo solemnly presented the thimble, saying "We beg your acceptance of this elegant thimble"; y, when it had finished this short speech, they all cheered.

Alicia pensó la whole cosa muy absurda, pero they all looked so grave that she did not dare to laugh; y, as she could not pensar of algo to say, she simply bowed, y took the thimble, looking as solemne as ella could.

La next cosa was to eat the comfits: this caused some noise y confusión, as the large pájaros complained that they could not taste theirs, y the small ones choked y had to be patted on the back. Pero, it was over at last, y they sat down otra vez en un ring, y beggeó al Ratón to tell them algo más.

"You promised to tell me tu historia, tú sabes," dijo Alicia, "y why it is you hate—C y D," ella agregó en un whisper, half afraid que it would be offended otra vez.

"Mine is a long y a sad tale!" dijo el Ratón, turneando hacia Alicia, y sighing.

"It *is* a long tail, certainly," dijo Alicia, looking down con wonder al Ratón's tail; "pero why do you call it sad?" Y ella kept on puzzling about it mientras el Ratón estaba speakeando, so that her idea of the tale era algo así:—

        "Fury dijo to
          a ratón, That
            he met in the
              casa, 'Let
                us both go
                  to law: *I*
                    will prose-
                    cute *you*.—
                Come, I'll
              take no de-
            nial: We
          must have
        the trial;
      For de veras
     this morn-
    ing I've
    nada
    to do.'
      Dijo el
        ratón to
          the cur,
            'Such a
              trial, dear
                sir, With
                  no jury
                  or judge,
                would
              waste
            nuestro
          breath.'
        'I'll be
      juez,
    y ju-
    rado,'
    dijo
    cun-
      ning
        old
          Fury;
          'I'll
           try
           the
           whole
         cause,
       and
     con-
    demn
  you a
 muerte.'

"You are not attending!" dijo el Ratón a Alicia severamente. "What are you pensando of?"

"I beg your perdón," dijo Alicia very humblemente: "you had got to the fifth bend, yo pienso?"

"I had *not!*" gritó el Ratón, sharply y muy angrily.

"A knot!" dijo Alicia, always ready to make herself useful, y looking anciosamente about her. "Oh, do let me ayudar to undo it!"

"I shall do nada of the sort," dijo el Ratón, getting up y walking away. "You insult me by hablando tantas tonterías!"

"I didn't mean it!" pleadeó la pobre Alicia. "Pero you're so easily offended, tú sabes!"

El Ratón only growleó en respuesta.

"Por favor come back y finish your story!" Alicia called after it; y the others all joined en coro, "Yes, por favor do!" pero el Ratón solo shooqueó su cabeza impacientemente, y caminó un poquito quicker.

"What a pity it wouldn't stay!" sighed el Lory, as soon as it was quite out of sight; y an old Crab took the opportunity of saying to her daughter "Ah, my dear! Let this be una lección to you never to lose *your* temper!"

"Hold your lengua, Ma!" dijo el young Crab, un poquito snappishly. "You're enough to try the patience of an oyster!"

"I wish I had our Dinah here, I know I do!" dijo Alicia aloud, addressing nobody in particular. "She'd soon fetch it back!"

"Y who is Dinah, if I might venture to ask la cuestión?" dijo el Lory.

Alicia replicó eagerly, for she was always ready to talk about her pet: "Dinah es nuestro gato. Y she's such a capital one for catching ratones you can't think! Y oh, I wish you could see her after los pájaros! Why, she'll eat un little pajarito as soon as look at it!"

Este speech caused a remarcable sensación among el grupo. Some of los pájaros hurried off a la vez: one old Magpie began wrapping itself up muy carefully, remarcando, "Yo de veras must be getting home; the night-air doesn't suit my throat!" y a Canary called out en una trembling voz to its children, "Come away, my dears! It's high tiempo you were all in bed!" On various pretexts they all moved off, y Alicia was soon left alone.

"I wish I hadn't mentioned Dinah!" ella dijo pa'sí misma in a melancholy tono. "Nobody seems to like her, down here, y I'm sure she's el major gato del mundo! Oh, my dear Dinah! I wonder if I shall ever see you any more!" Y here pobre Alicia began to cry otra vez, for she felt muy lonely y low-spirited. En un little while, pero, ella otra vez oyó un little pattering of footsteps en la distancia, y ella looked up eagerly, half hopeando que el Ratón había cambiado su mente, y was coming back pa'terminar el cuento.

El Rabit Manda una Pequeña Bill

Era el Rabit Blanco, trotteando slowly back otra vez, y looking anciosamente about as it went, as if it had lost algo; y ella heard it muttering to itself "La Duquesa! La Duquesa! Oh my dear paws! Oh my fur y whiskers! She'll get me executed, as sure as ferrets are ferrets! Where *can* I have dropped them, I wonder?" Alicia guessed en un momento que it was looking for el fan y the pair of white kid guantes, y she muy good-naturedly began hunteando about por ellos, pero they were nowhere to ser vistos—todo seemed to have cambiado since her swim en la pool, y the great hall, with the glass table y la little puertita, had vanished completely.

Muy soon el Rabit notice a Alicia as she went hunteando about, y called out to her en un angry tono, "Why, Mary Ann, what *are* you doing out here? Run home this momento, y fetch me a pair of guantes y a fan! Quick, now!" Y Alicia was so mucho frightened that she ran off at once in the dirección it pointed to, without trying to explain the mistake it had made.

"He took me por su sirvienta," ella dijo pa'sí misma as she ran. "How surprised he'll be when he finds out who I am! Pero I'd better take him his fan y guantes—that is, if I can find them." Mientras decía esto, she came upon una neat little casita, on the puerta of which was a bright brass plate with the name "RABIT B." engraveada en ella. She went in sin knoquear, y hurrideó upstairs, en great miedo lest ella should meet a la real Mary Ann, y be turned out of the casa before she had found el fan y guantes.

"How extraño it seems," Alicia dijo pa'sí misma, "to be transportando mensajes pa'un rabit! I suppose Dinah'll be sending me mensajes next!" Y ella began fancying the sort of cosa that would happen: "'Miss Alicia! Come here directly, y get ready for your walk!' 'Coming in un minuto, nurse! Pero tengo que ver que el ratón doesn't get out.' Only I don't think," Alicia siguió, "that they'd let Dinah stop en la casa if it began ordenando people about de esa manera!"

Para este momento she had found her way into un tidy little cuartito with una mesa en la ventana, y on it (as she had hoped) a fan y two or three pairs of tiny white kid guantes: she took up el fan y a pair of the guantes, y was just going to leave the room, when su ojo fell upon una little botellita that stood cerca del looking-glass. There was no label this time with the words "DRINQUÉAME", pero nevertheless she uncorked it y put it to her lips.

"I know *algo* interesting is sure to happen," ella dijo pa'sí misma, "whenever I eat or drinque cualquier cosa; so I'll just see what esta botella does. I do hope it'll make me grow grande otra vez, for de veras I'm quite cansada de being such a tiny cosita!"

Lo hizo así indeed, y mucho sooner de lo que ella había expecteado: before she had tomado half la botella, ella found su cabeza pressing against el techo, y tuvo que stoop pa'salvar su cuello from being roto. She hasteamente put down the la botella, saying pa'sí misma "That's quite enough—I hope I sha'n't grow any more—As it is, I can't get out at la puerta—I do wish I hadn't drunk quite so mucho!"

Alas! it was too tarde to wish eso! She went on growing, y growing, y muy soon had to kneel down on the floor: in another minuto no había room pa'esto, y ella tried the effect of lying down with one codo against la puerta, y el otro brazo curleado round su cabeza. Still she went on growing, y, como un último resource, she put un brazo fuera de la ventana, y one foot up la chimenea, y dijo pa'sí misma "Now I can do no more, whatever happens. What *will* become of me?"

Luckily for Alicia, la little magic botellita had ahora had its full effect, y ella grew no larger: still it was muy uncomfortable, y, as there seemed to be no sort of chance of her ever getting out del cuarto otra vez, no wonder she felt unhappy.

"Era mucho más pleasanter en casa," pensó la pobre Alicia, "when one wasn't always growing larger y smaller, y being ordered about by ratones y rabits. I casi wish I hadn't gone down that rabit-hoyo—y yet—y yet—it's algo curious, tú sabes, this sort of vida! I do wonder what *can* have happened a mí! Cuando yo solía leer fairy-cuentos, I fancied that kind of cosa never happened, y ahora aquí I am en medio de of one! There ought to be a book written about me, that there ought! Y cuando I grow up, I'll write one—pero I'm grown up ahora," she added in a sorrowful tono; "al menos there's no espacio pa'crecer up any more *aquí*."

"Pero entonces," pensó Alicia, "shall I *never* get any older than I am ahora? That'll be a comfort, one way—never to be an old woman—pero then—always to have lecciones to learn! Oh, I shouldn't like *that*!"

"Oh, you foolish Alicia!" she answered herself. "How can you learn lecciones in here? Why, there's hardly room for *you*, y no room at all for any lección-books!"

Y so she went on, taking first one side y then the other, y making quite a conversación of it altogether; pero after unos minutos ella oyó una voz outside, y stopped a escuchar.

"Mary Ann! Mary Ann!" dijo la voz. "Fetch me my guantes this momento!" Then came a little pattering of feet on the stairs. Alicia knew it was the Rabit coming to look for her, y ella trembleó till ella shook la casa, quite forgeteando que ella was ahora about a thousand veces as large as the Rabit, y had no reason to be afraid of it.

Presentemente el Rabit came up to the door, y tried to open it; pero, as the door opened inwards, y Alicia's elbow was pressed hard against it, that attempt proved a failure. Alicia heard it say to itself "Then I'll go round y get in por la ventana."

"*Eso* you wo'n't," pensó Alicia, y, después de esperar till she fancied she heard the Rabit justo bajo su ventana, ella suddenly spreadeó out su mano, y made a snatch en el aire. She did not agarró nada, pero she heard un pequeño shriek y una caída, y un crash de broken vidrio, del cual ella concluyó que era un poquito possible it had fallen en un cucumber-frame, or algo así.

Next vino una angry voz—la del Rabit—-"João! João! Where estás tú?" Y luego una voz she had never heard antes, "Pois then I'm acá! Diggeando por manzanas, senhor!"

"Diggeando por manzana, indeed!" dijo el Rabit, que estaba enojado. "Here! Ven y help me out de *esto*!" (Sonidos de más broken glass.)

"Now tell a mí, João, what's that en la ventana?"

"Pois, it's un braço, senhor!" (Él pronounced it "brazu.")

"Un brazo, you ganso! Who ever saw una de ese tamaño? Why, it fills la whole ventana!"

"Pois, it does, senhor: pero it's un braço despois de todo."

"Bien, it's got ningún business allá, at any rato: ve y take it away!"

Hubo un largo silencio after this, y Alicia could only hear whispers now y then; such as, "Sure, I don't like it, senhor, at all, at all!" "Do como te digo, you coward!" y at last she spread out her hand otra vez, y made another snatch in the air. This tiempo there were *dos* pequeños shrieks, y more sounds of broken glass. "What a number of cucumber-frames there must be!" pensó Alicia. "I wonder what they'll do next! As for pulling me out de la ventana, I only wish they *could*! I'm sure I don't want to stay in here any longer!"

She waited for some tiempo without escuchando algo más: at last came a rumbling of little cartwheels, y el sonido de a good many voces all talking together: she made out las palabras: "Where's the other ladder?—Why, I hadn't to bring pero one; Bill's got the other—Bill! fetch it here, lad!—Here, put 'em up at esta esquina—No, tie 'em together first—they don't reach half high enough todavía—Oh! they'll do bien enough; don't be particular—Here, Bill! catch hold of this rope—Will the roof bear?—Mind that loose slate—Oh, it's coming down! Heads below!" (A loud crash.) "Now, who did that?—It was Bill, I fancy—Who's to go down la chimenea?—Nay, I sha'n't! *You* do it!—That I wo'n't, then!—Bill's to go down—Here, Bill! the master says you're to go down la chimenea!"

"Oh! So Bill's got to come down la chimenea, has he?" dijo Alicia pa'sí misma. "Shy, they seem to put todo upon Bill! I wouldn't be in Bill's place for a good deal: this fireplace is narrow, to be sure; pero yo *pienso* I can kick un poco!"

She drew her foot as far down la chimenea as she could, y waited till she heard un little animalit (she couldn't guess of what sort it was) scratcheando y scrambleando about en la chimenea close above her: then, saying pa'sí misma "Este es

Bill," she gave one sharp patada, y waited to see what would happen next.

The first cosa she heard was a general coro of "There goes Bill!" then el Rabit's voz along—"Catch him, you by the hedge!" then silence, y then another confusión de voces—"Hold up su cabeza—Brandy now—Don't choke him—How was it, old fellow? What happened to you? Tell us all about it!"

Al final came una little feeble, squeakeante voz, ("That's Bill," pensó Alicia,) "Bien, I hardly sé—No más, thank ye; I'm better ahora—pero I'm a deal too flustered to tell you—all I know is, algo comes at me like a Jack-in-the-box, and up I goes like a sky-rocket!"

"So you did, old fellow!" dijeron los demás.

"We must burn la casa down!" dijo la Rabit's voz; y Alicia called out as loud as she could, "If you do. I'll set Dinah at you!"

There was a dead silence instantly, y Alicia pensó pa'sí misma, "I wonder what they *will* do next! If they had any sense, they'd take the roof off." After un minuto or two, they empezaron a moverse about otra vez, y Alicia heard el Rabit decir, "A barrowful will do, to begin with."

"A barrowful de *qué?*" pensó Alicia; pero she had not long pa'dudar, for the next momento a shower of little pebbelitos came rattling in a la ventana, y some of them hit her en la cara. "I'll put un stop a esto," ella dijo pa'sí misma, y shouted out, "Tú better not do eso otra vez!" which produced another dead silence.

Alicia noticeó with some surprise that the pebbles were all turning into little pastelitos as they lay en el piso, y una bright idea came into su cabeza. "If I eat one of these cakes," she pensó, "it's sure to make *some* cambio in my size; y as it can't posiblemente make me larger, it must make me smaller, I suppose."

So she swallowed one of the cakes, y was delighted to find that she began shrinkeando directly. As soon as she was small enough to get through the door, ella corrió out de la casa, y found quite a crowd de little animalitos y pájaros waiting afuera. La pobre little Lizard, Bill, was in the middle, being held up by two guinea-puercos, who were giving it algo out of la botella. They all made a rush at Alicia el momento she appeared; pero she ran off as hard as she could, y soon found herself a salvo in a thick wood.

"La first cosa I've got to do," dijo Alicia pa'sí misma, mientras ella wandereaba about en el wood, "is to crecer a mi right size otra vez; y la second cosa is to find my way into that lovely jardín. Yo pienso that will be the best plan."

It sounded un excellent plan, no doubt, y muy neatly y simply arranged; la única dificultad was, that she had not the smallest idea how to set about it; y while she was peereando about anciosamente among the trees, a little sharp bark just over su cabeza made her look up en una great hurry.

Un enormous perrito was looking down at her con large round ojos, y feeblemente stretching out one paw, trying to touch her. "Pobre little cosita!" dijo Alicia, in a coaxing tono, y ella tried hard to chiflarle; pero ella estaba terriblemente frighteneada todo el tiempo at the pensamiento that it might be hungry, in which case it would be muy likely de comérsela in spite of all her coaxing.

Hardly sabiendo qué había hecho, ella piqueó up a little bit of stick, y held it out to el perrito; whereupon el perrito jumped into the air off all its feet At once, with a yelp of delight, y rushed at the stick, y made believe to worry it; then Alicia dodged behind a great thistle, to keep herself from being run over; y el momento she appeared on the other side, el perrito made another rush at the stick, y tumbled cabeza over heels en su hurry to get hold of it; then Alicia, pensando it was mucho like having un juego of play with a cart-horse, y expecting every momento to be trampled under sus pies, ran round el thistle otra vez; then el perrito began a series of short cambios at the stick, running a very little way forwards cada tiempo y a long way back, y barking hoarsely all the while, till at last it sat down a good way off, panting, with su lengua hanging out de su boca, y con great ojos half shut.

This seemed to Alicia a good opportunity for making her escape; so she set off at once, y ran till she was quite cansada y out of respiración, y till el perrito's bark sounded quite faint in the distance.

"Y yet what un dear little perrito it was!" dijo Alicia, as she leant against a buttercup to rest herself, y fanned herself con una de las leaves: "Me hubiera gustado teaching it tricks very much, if—if I'd only been the right size to do it! Oh dear! Yo casi me olvidaba que I've got to grow up otra vez! Let me ver—cómo *is* it to be managed? Supongoq ue I ought to comer o drinquear algo or other; pero la great cuestión es, qué?"

La great cuestión certainly era, what? Alicia looked all round her at the flowers y the blades de pasto, pero she no vio nada that looked like the right cosa to comer or drinquear under las circumstancias. There was a large mushroom growing near her, about the same height as herself; y when she had looked under it, y on both sides of it, y behind it, it occurred to her that she might igualmente look y see what was on the top of it.

She stretched herself up on tiptoe, y peeped over the edge of the mushroom, y sus ojos inmediatamente met those of a large Caterpilar, that was sitting on the top with sus brazos folded, quietly smoking a long hookah, y taking not the smallest noticia of her or de nada más.

Consejo del Caterpilar

El Caterpilar y Alicia se vieron at each other for some tiempo en silencio: at last the Caterpilar took the hookah out of its mouth, y addressed her in a languid, sleepy voz.

"Who are *you?*" dijo el Caterpilar.

This was not an encouraging opening for a conversación. Alicia replicó, algo shyly, "I—I hardly know, sir, just at present—al menos I know quién I *was* cuando me desperté this morning, pero yo pienso I must have been cambiada varias veces since entonces."

"What do you mean by that?" dijo el Caterpilar sterneamente. "Explain yourself!"

"I can't explain *myself*, I'm afraid, sir," dijo Alicia, "because I'm not myself, you see."

"I don't see," dijo el Caterpilar.

"I'm afraid I can't put it more clearly," Alicia replicó muy politely, "for I can't understand it myself to begin with; y being tantos tamaños diferentes en un día is muy confusing."

"It isn't," dijo el Caterpilar.

"Bien, quizás you haven't found it so todavía," dijo Alicia; "pero when you have to turn into a chrysalis—you will un día, tú sabes—y then after that into una mariposa, I should think you'll feel it un poquito extraño, wo'n't you?"

"Not a bit," dijo el Caterpilar.

"Bien, perhaps your feelings pueden ser diferentes," dijo Alicia; "all I know is, it would feel muy extraño to *me*."

"You!" dijo el Caterpilar contemptuousamente. "Who are *you*?"

Which brought them back otra vez to the beginning de la conversación. Alicia felt un poquito irritada porque el Caterpilar estaba making such *very* short remarcas, y ella drew herself hacia arriba y dijo, muy gravemente, "Yo pienso, you ought to tell me quién *tú* eres, first."

"Por qué?" dijo el Caterpilar.

Here was another puzzling cuestión; y as Alicia could not pensar of any good reason, y as the Caterpilar seemed to be in a *muy* unpleasant state of mind, she turned away.

"Come back!" the Caterpilar called after her. "Tengo algo importante to say!"

This sounded promising, certainly: Alicia turned y came back otra vez.

"Keep your temper," dijo el Caterpilar.

"Eso es todo?" dijo Alicia, swallowing down her anger as bien as she could.

"No," dijo el Caterpilar.

Alicia pensó she might mejor esperar, as she had nada más to do, y perhaps after all it might tell her algo worth hearing. For some minutos it puffed away without speaking, pero at last it unfolded its brazos, took the hookah out of its mouth otra vez, y dijo, "So you think you're cambiado, do you?"

"I'm afraid I am, sir," dijo Alicia; "I can't remembrear cosas as I used—y I don't keep the same size por diez minutos together!"

"Can't remembrear *what* cosas?" dijo el Caterpilar.

"Bien, I've tried to decir '*Cómo Doth the Little Busy Bee*', pero it all came diferente!" Alicia replicó en una muy melancholy voz.

"Repeat, '*You are Old, Padre Guillermo*'," dijo el Caterpilar.

Alicia folded sus manos, y empezó:—

"You are old, Padre Guillermo," el young man said,
  "Y your pelo has become muy white;
Y yet you incessantly stand on your head—
  Do you piensas, at your edad, it is right?"

"In my youth," Padre Guillermo replicó to his son,
  "I feared it might injure el brain;
Pero, now that I'm perfectly sure I have none,
  Why, lo hago otra vez y again."

"You are old," dijo el youth, "as I mentioned before,
  Y have grown muy uncommonly fat;
Yet you turned a back-somersault in at the door—
  Pray, what is la reazón of that?"

"In my youth," dijo el sage, as he shook sus grey locks,
  "I kept all my limbs muy supple
By the use of this ointment—one shilling the box—
  Allow me to sell you a couple?"

"You are old," dijo el youth, "y your jaws son muy weak
  Para algo tougher que suet;
Yet you finished the goose, con los bones y el beak—
  Pray cómo tu managed to do it?"

"En mi youth," dijo el padre, "I took to the law,
  Y argued each caso con mi wife;
Y la muscular strength, which it gave to my jaw,
  Has lasted el rest de mi life."

"You are old," dijo el youth, "one would hardly suppose
    That your ojo was as steady as ever;
Yet you balanced un eel on el end de tu nose—
    What made you tan awfully clever?"

"I have answered three cuestiones, y eso is enough,"
    Dijo su father; "don't give yourself airs!
Do you think I can listen all dia to such stuff?
    Be off, or I'll kick you down stairs!"

"That is not said correctamente," dijo el Caterpilar.

"Not *quite* right, I'm afraid," dijo Alicia, timidamente; "some of the words have got altered."

"It is wrong from beginning to end," dijo el Caterpilar decididamente, y there was silence for some minutos.

El Caterpilar was the first to speak.

"What size do you want to be?" it asked.

"Oh, I'm not particular as to size," Alicia hastily replicó; "only one doesn't like changing so often, tú sabes."

"I *don't* know," dijo el Caterpilar.

Alicia dijo nada: she had never been so much contradicteada en su vida before, y ella felt that she was losing her temper.

"Are you content ahora?" dijo el Caterpilar.

"Bien, I should like to be a *little* larger, sir, if you wouldn't mind," dijo Alicia: "tres inches es such a wretched height to be."

"Es a muy good height indeed!" dijo el Caterpilar enojado, rearing itself upright mientras hablaba (it was exactly tres inches high).

"Pero I'm not used to it!" pleadeó la pobre Alicia in a piteous tono. Y ella pensó of herself, "I wish las criaturas wouldn't be so fácilmente ofendidas!"

"You'll get used to it a tiempo," dijo el Caterpilar; y it put the hookah into its mouth y began fumando otra vez.

This tiempo Alicia waited pacientemente until it chose to speak otra vez. In un minuto or two el Caterpilar tomó the hookah out of its mouth y yawned once or twice, y shook itself. Then it got down off the mushroom, y crawled away en el pasto, merely remarcando as it went, "One side will make you grow taller, y the other side will make you grow shorter."

"One side of *what*? The other side of *what*?" pensó Alicia pa'sí misma.

"Of the mushroom," dijo Caterpilar, just as if she had asked it aloud; y in another momento it was out of sight.

Alicia siguió looking thoughtfully al mushroom por un minuto, tratando to make out cuáles eran sus dos lados; y as it was perfectamente redondo, she found this una cuestión muy dificil. Pero, at last she stretched sus brazos round it as far as they would go, y broke off a bit of the edge with each mano.

"Y ahora which is which?" ella dijo pa'sí misma, y nibbled a little of the right-hand bit to try el efecto: the next momento she felt un golpe violento underneath her barbilla: it had struck her foot!

Ella estaba a good deal frightened por este muy sudden cambio, pero she felt that there was no tiempo to be lost, as she was shrinking rapidamente; so she set to work at once to eat some of the other bit. Her chin was pressed so closely against her foot, that there was hardly room to open her mouth; pero she did it at last, y managed to swallowear una morsel of the lefthand bit.

*   *   *   *   *

*   *   *   *

*   *   *   *   *

"Come, mi cabeza's free at last!" dijo Alicia in a tono of delight, which cambió into alarma en another momento, when she found que sus hombros were nowhere to be found: all she could see, when she looked down, was an immense length of neck, which seemed to rise like a stalk out of a sea of green leaves that lay far below her.

"What *can* all that green stuff be?" dijo Alicia. "Y dónde *have* mis hombros got to? Y oh, mis pobres manos, how is it I can't see you?" She was moving them about as she spoke, pero no result seemed to follow, except a little shaking among the distant green leaves.

As there seemed to be no chance of getting sus manos up to su cabeza, she tried to get su cabeza down to them, y was delighted to find that her neck would bend about easily in any dirección, like a serpiente. She had just succeeded in curving it down into a graceful zigzag, y was going to dive in among the leaves, which she found to be nada pero the tops of the trees under which she had been wandering, when a sharp hiss made her draw back in a hurry: un gran pigeon había flowneado into su cara, y was beating her violently with its wings.

"Serpiente!" gritó el Pigeon.

"I'm *not* a serpiente!" dijo Alicia indignantly. "Let me alone!"

"Serpiente, I say otra vez!" repitió el Pigeon, pero in a more subdued tono, y added with a kind of sob, "I've tried every way, y nada seems to suit them!"

"I haven't the least idea what you're talking about," dijo Alicia.

"I've tried the roots of trees, y I've tried banks, y I've tried hedges," el Pigeon went on, without attending a ella; "pero those serpientes! There's no pleasing them!"

Alicia was more y more puzzled, pero ella pensó there was no use en decir cualquier cosa more hasta que el Pigeon had finished.

"As if it wasn't trouble enough hatching los huevos," dijo el Pigeon; "pero I must be on the look-out for serpientes noche y día! Why, no he tenido un wink de sleep estas tres semanas three!"

"I'm muy sorry que tú estás annoyed," dijo Alicia, que estaba empezando a ver its meaning.

"Y just as I'd taken the highest árbol en el wood," continuó el Pigeon, raiseando su voz to a shriek, "y just as I was pensando I should estar libre of them at last, they must needs come wriggling down from tel cielo! Ugh, Serpiente!"

"Pero I'm *not* una serpiente, I tell you!" dijo Alicia. "I'm a—I'm a—"

"Bien! *Qué* are you?" dijo el Pigeon. "I can see you're trying to invent algo!"

"I—I'm una little niñita," dijo Alicia, algo doubtfully, as she remembreó el número de cambios she had gone through ese día.

"A likely story indeed!" dijo el Pigeon in a tono of the deepest contempt. "I've seen a good muchas little niñas in my tiempo, pero never *one* with such a neck as that! No, no! You're a serpiente; y there's no use denying it. I suppose you'll be telling me next that you never tasted a huevo!"

"I *have* tasted huevos, certainly," dijo Alicia, que era una muy truthful niña; "pero little niñas comen huevos quite as much as las serpientes do, tú sabes."

"I don't believe it," dijo el Pigeon; "pero if they do, why then they're a kind of serpiente, eso es todo lo que puedo decir."

This was such a new idea to Alicia, that she was quite silent por un minuto or two, which gave al Pigeon la oportunidad de agregar, "You're looking for huevos, I know *that* bien enough; y what does it matter a mí si you're a little niña or a serpiente?"

"It matters a good deal to *me*," dijo Alicia hastily; "pero I'm not looking for huevos, as it happens; y if I was, I shouldn't want *yours*: I don't like them raw."

"Bien, be off, entonces!" dijo el Pigeon in a sulky tono, mientras se settle\aba down otra vez dentro de su nest. Alicia croucheó down entre los árboles tan bien como she pudo, for su cuello kept getting entangleado among las branches, y every now y luego she had to detenerse y untwistearlo. Luego de un rato ella remembreó que ella still held los pedazos de mushroom en sus manos, y ella set to work muy carefully, nibbling first at one y then at the other, y growing sometimes taller y sometimes shorter, until she had succeeded in bringing herself down to her usual height.

It was so long desde que she had been algo near the right size, that it felt quite extraño at first; pero she got used to it en unos few minutos, y began talkeando pa'sí misma, as usual. "Come, there's half my plan done now! How puzzling all these cambios are! I'm never sure what I'm going to be, from one minuto to another! Pero, I've got back to my right size: the next cosa es, to get into that beautiful jardín—how *is* that to be done, I wonder?" Mientras decía esto, she came suddenly upon an open place, con una little casa in it about cuatro feet alta. "Whoever vive there," pensó Alicia, "it'll never do to come upon ellos en *esta* size: why, yo los debo frightenear them out de sus wits!" So ella empezó a nibbler at la righthand bit otra vez, y did not venture to go cerca de la casa till she had brought herself down a nueve inches high.

C A P Í T U L O   V I

P i g   y   P e p e r

Por un minuto or two ella stood looking a la casa, and wondering what to do next, when suddenly a footman in livery came running out of the wood—(she considered him to be a footman because he was in livery: otherwise, judging solo por su cara, she would have called him a fish)—y rapped loudly at la puerta with his knuckles. It was abierta by another footman in livery, con una roud cara, y large ojos like una rana; y both footmen, Alicia noticed, had powdered pero que curled all over sus cabezas. She felt muy curiosa to know what it was all about, y crept a little way out of the wood to listen.

El Fish-Footman began by producing from under su brazo a great carta, nearly as large as himself, y this he handed over to the other, saying, in a solemn tono, "Para la Duquesa. An invitación from la Reina to play croqueta." El Frog-Footman repitió, in the same solemne tono, only changing the order of the words a little, "De la Reina. Una invitación para la Duquesa a jugar croqueta."

Then they both bowed low, y their curls got entangled together.

Alicia laughed so much at this, that she had to run back into the wood for fear of their hearing her; y when she next peeped out the Fish-Footman was gone, y the other was sitting on the ground cerca de la puerta, staring estúpidamente up hacia el cielo.

Alicia went timidamente up to la puerta, y knoqueó.

"There's no sort of use in knocking," dijo el Footman, "y that for two reasons. First, porque I'm on the same side de la puerta as you are; secondly, porque they're making such a ruido inside, no one could posiblemente hear you." Y certainly there was a most extraordinary noise going on within—a constant howling y sneezing, y every now y then a great crash, as if a dish or kettle had been broken to pedazos.

"Por favor, then," dijo Alicia, "how am I to get in?"

"There might be some sense in your knocking," el Footman went on without attending to her, "if we had la puerta between us. Por ejemplo, if you were *inside*, you might knock, y I could let you out, tú sabes." He was looking up into the sky all the tempo él estaba speaking, y esto Alicia pensó que era decididamente uncivil. "Pero quizás he can't help it," ella dijo pa'sí misma; "sus ojos are so *very* nearly at the top of su cabeza. Pero at any rate he might answer cuestiones.—How am I to get in?" ella repitió, aloud.

"I shall sit here," el Footman remarcó, "till tomorrow—"

At this momento la puerta de la casa opened, y a large plate came skimming out, straight al Footman's cabeza: it just grazed his nose, y broke to pedazos against one of the trees behind him.

"—or next día, maybe," el Footman continued in the same tono, exactly as if nada had happened.

"How am I to get in?" asked Alicia otra vez, in a louder tono.

"*Are* you to get in at all?" dijo el Footman. "That's la first cuestión, tú sabes."

It was, no doubt: only Alicia did not like to be told so. "It's súper dreadful," she muttered pa'sí misma, "the way todas las criaturas argue. It's enough to drive one crazy!"

El Footman seemed to pensar this a good opportunity for repeating his remarca, with variaciones. "I shall sit here," él dijo, "on y off, por días y días."

"Pero what am I to do?" dijo Alicia.

"Algo you like," dijo el Footman, y began whistling.

"Oh, there's no use in talking to him," dijoe Alicia desesperadamente: "he's perfectly idiotic!" Y she opened la puerta y went in.

La puerta led right into a large kitchen, which was full of smoke from one end to the other: la Duquesa was sitting on a three-legged stool in the middle, nursing a baby; el cocinero was leaning over the fire, stirring a large cauldron which seemed to be full of soup.

"There's certainly too much pepper in that soup!" Alicia dijo pa'sí misma, tan bien como ella could for sneezing.

There was certainly too much of it in the air. Even la Duquesa sneezed occasionally; y as for the baby, it was sneezing y howling alternately without a momento's pause. The only cosas in the kitchen que did not sneeze, were el cocinero, y a large cat which was sitting on the corazón y grinning from ear to ear.

"Por favor would you decirme," dijo Alicia, a little tímidamente, for she was not quite sure whether it was good manners for her to speak first, "why your gato grins like that?"

"Es un Gato de Cheshire," dijo la Duquesa, "y that's why. Pig!"

Ella dijo la última palabra with such sudden violence que Alicia quite jumped; pero she saw in another momento que it was addressed to the baby, y not to her, so she took coraje, y went on otra vez:—

"I didn't know que los gatos de Cheshire siempre grinnean; in facto, yo no sabía que los gatos *pudieran* grinear."

"They all can," dijo la Duquesa; "y most of 'em do."

"I don't know of any that do," Alicia dijo muy politely, feeling quite pleaseda to have metida into una conversación.

"You don't know mucho," dijo la Duquesa; "y that's un facto."

Alicia did not at all like el tono de esta remarca, y pensó que it would be igual to introducir some otros sujectos de conversación. While she was trying to fix on one, el cocinero took the cauldron de sopa off el fuego, e inmediatamente set to work throwing todo within her reach a la Duquesa y el baby—the fire-irons came first; then followed a shower of saucepans, plates, y dishes. La Duquesa tomó no notice of them even when they hit her; y el baby was howling so much already, que it was quite imposible to say whether the blows hurt it or not.

"Oh, *por favor* mindeao what you're haciendo!" cried Alicia, saltando up y down en una agony de terror. "Oh, allí va his *precious* nariz"; as an unusually largo saucepan flew cerca, y muy nearly carried it off.

"If everybody minded their own business," la Duquesa dijo en un hoarse growl, "the world would go round a deal faster than it does."

"Which would *not* be una ventaja," dijo Alicia, who felt muy contenta to get an opportunity of showing off un poquito de su knowledge. "Just think of what work it would make with the day y night! You see la tierra takes twenty-four horas to turn round on su axis—"

"Talking of axes," dijo la Duquesa, "chop off su cabeza!"

Alicia glanced algo anciosamente at el cocinero, to see if she meant to take the hint; pero el cocinero was busily stirring the soup, y seemed not to be listening, so ella went on otra vez: "Twenty-four horas, yo *pienso*; or is it doce? I—"

"Oh, don't bother *me*," dijo la Duquesa; "I never could abide figures!" Y with that she began nursing her child otra vez, singing a sort of lullaby to it as she did so, y giving it a violent shake at the end of every line:—

> *"Espeak roughly a tu little boy,*
> *Y beat him cuando él sneezes:*
> *Él solo does it to annoy,*
> *Porque él knows it teases."*

Coro
(in which el cook y el baby joined):—
"Guou! guou! guou!"

Mientras la Duquesa cantaba the second verse of la canción, she kept tossing the baby violently up y down, y la pobre little cosita howled so, que Alicia could hardly oir las palabras:—

> *"Yo espeak severamente to my boy,*
> *I beat him cuando él sneezes;*
> *For él can thoroughly enjoy*
> *El peper cuando él pleases!"*

CORO
"Guou! guou! guou!"

"Here! you may nurse it a bit, if you like!" la Duquesa dijo a Alicia, flinging the baby at her as she spoke. "I must go y get ready to play croqueta con la Reina," y ella hurridió out del room. The cocinero threw a frying-pan after her as she went out, pero it just missed her.

Alicia caught al baby with some dificultad, as it was a extraño-shaped little criaturita, y held out sus brazos y piernas in all direcciones, "just like a star-fish," pensó Alicia. La pobre little cosita was snorting like a steam-engine when she caught it, y kept doubling itself up y straightening itself out otra vez, so that altogether, por el first minuto or two, it was as much as she could do to hold it.

As soon as she had made out the proper way of nursing it, (which was to twist it up into a sort of knot, y then keep tight hold of its right ear y left foot, so as to prevent its undoing itself,) she carried it out into the open air. "*If* I don't take this child away conmigo," pensó Alicia, "they're sure to kill it in un día o dos: wouldn't it be murder to leave it behind?" Ella dijo las últimas palabras out loud, y la little cosita grunteó in reply (it had left off sneezing by este tiempo). "Don't grunt," dijo Alicia; "that's not at all a proper way of expressing yourself."

El baby grunteó otra vez, y Alicia looked muy anciosamente into su cara to see what was the matter with it. There could be no doubt que it had a *muy* turn-up nariz, much more like a snout than a real nose; also sus ojos were getting extremely small for a baby: altogether a Alicia no le gusto el look de la cosa at all. "Pero perhaps it was only sobbing," ella pensó, y looked into sus ojos otra vez, to see if there were any tears.

No, there were no tears. "If you're going to turn into a pig, my dear," dijo Alicia, seriously, "I'll have nada more to do with you. Mind now!" La pobre little cosita sobbed otra vez (or grunted, it was imposible to say cuál), y they went on for some while in silence.

Alicia was just beginning to pensar pa'sí misma, "Now, what am I to do with this creature when I get it home?" when it grunteó otra vez, so violentamente, que she looked down into su cara con some alarma. This tiempo there could be *no* mistake about it: it was neither more nor less than a pig, y ella felt que it would be quite absurd for her to carry it further.

So she set the little criaturita down, y felt quite relieved to see it trot away quietly into the wood. "If it had grown up," ella dijo pa'sí misma, "it would have made a dreadfully ugly child: pero it makes alo de un handsome pig, yo pienso." Y ella empezó thinking over other niños she knew, who might

do muy bien as pigs, y was just saying pa'sí misma, "if one only knew the right way to cambiarlos—" when she was un poquito startled de seeing el Gato de Cheshire sentado on a bough of a tree a few yards off.

El Gato solamente grinneó when it saw Alicia. It looked good-natured, ella pensó: still tenía *muy* long claws y a great muchos teeth, so she felt que it ought to be treated with respect.

"Cheshire Puss," ella empezó, aldo tímida, as she did not at all know whether it would like the name: pero, it only grinned un poquito widdlyer. "Come, it's pleasedo so far," pensó Alicia, y ella went on. "Would you decirme, por favor, which way I ought to ir de aquí?"

"That depends a good deal on where you want to get to," dijo el Gato.

"I don't much care where—" dijo Alicia.

"Then it doesn't matter which way you go," dijo Gato.

"—so long as I get *somewhere*," Alicia added as an explanación.

"Oh, you're sure to do that," dijo el Gato, "if you only walk long enough."

Alicia felt que this could not be denied, so she tried otra cuestión. "What sort of people live about here?"

"In *that* dirección," el Gato dijo, waving its right paw round, "vive el Hatter: y in *that* dirección," waving la otra paw, "vive una March Hare. Visit either si tu quieres: they're both locos."

"Pero I don't want to go among loco people," Alicia remarcó.

"Oh, you can't help that," dijo el Gato: "we're all loco aquí. I'm loco. You're loca."

"How do you know I'm loca?" dijo Alicia.

"You must be," dijo el Gato, "or you wouldn't have venido aquí."

Alicia didn't think that proved it at all; pero, she went on "Y how do you know que you're loco?"

"To begin with," dijo el Gato, "a dog's not loco. You grant that?"

"I suppose so," dijo Alicia.

"Bien, then," el Gato went on, "you see, un dog growlea when está angry, y wagea su tail when está pleaseado. Now I growleo when estoy pleasedo, y wageo mi tail cuando estoy angry. Therefore I'm loco."

"I call it purring, not growling," dijo Alicia.

"Call it what you like," dijo el Gato. "Do you play croqueta con la Reina to-day?"

"I should like it very mucho," dijo Alicia, "pero I haven't been invited yet."

"You'll see me there," dijo el Gato, y se vanisheó.

Alicia was not much surprised at this, she was getting so used to cosas extrañas happening. While she was looking at the place where it had been, it suddenly appeared otra vez.

"By-the-bye, what became of the baby?" dijo el Gato. "I'd nearly forgotten to ask."

"It turned into a pig," Alicia dijo quietly, just as if it had come back in a natural way.

"I thought it would," dijo el Gato, y vanished otra vez.

Alicia waited un poquito, half expecting a verlo otra vez, pero it did not appear, y after un minuto or two she walked on in the dirección in which la March Hare was said to live. "I've seen hatters antes," ella dijo pa'sí misma; "la March Hare will be much the most interesting, y perhaps as ahora es May it wo'n't be raving loco—at least no tan loco as it was en March." Mientras decía esto, she looked up, y allí estaba el Gato otra vez, sitteado en la brancha de un árbol.

"Did you say 'pig', or 'fig'?" dijo el Gato.

"Yo dije 'pig'," replicó Alicia; "y I wish you wouldn't keep appearing y vanishing so suddenly: you make one quite giddy."

"All right," dijo el Gato; y esta vez it vanished quite slowly, beginning with the end of the tail, y ending with the grin, which remained some tiempo after the rest of it had gone.

"Bien! I've often seen un gato sin un grin," pensó Alicia; "pero un grin sin un gato! It's la más curious cosa I ever saw en mi vida!"

Ella had not gone más lejos before ella came in sight de la casa de la March Hare: ella pensó it must be la casa correcta, porque las chimeneas were shaped like ears y the roof was thatched with fur. Era so grande a casa, que she did not like to go nearer till she had nibbled some more of the lefthand bit of mushroom, y raised herself to about two feet high: even then she walked up towards it rather timidamente, saying pa'sí misma "Suppose it should be raviando loco after all! I casi wish I'd gone a ver el Hatter instead!"

Un Tea-Party de Locos

Había una mesa set out under un árbol in front of la casa, y la March Hare y el Hatter were having tea at it: un Dormratón estaba sitting entre ellos, fast asleep, and the other two were using it as a cojín, resting their elbows on it, y talking over su cabeza. "Muy uncomfortable for the Dormratón," pensó Alicia; "only, as it's asleep, I suppose it doesn't mind."

The table was a large one, pero the three were all crowded together at one corner of it: "No room! No room!" they cried out when they saw Alicia coming. "There's *plenty* of room!" dijo Alicia indignantly, y ella sat down en una large brazo-chair at one final of the mesa.

"Have some wine," la March Hare dijo in an encouraging tono.

Alicia looked all round la mesa, pero there was nada on it pero tea. "I don't see any wine," she remarcó.

"There isn't any," dijo la March Hare.

"Then it wasn't muy civil of you to offer it," dijo Alicia angrily.

"It wasn't muy civil of you to sit down without being invited," dijo la March Hare.

"Yo no sabía que it was *your* mesa," dijo Alicia; "it's laid para a great muchos más than tres."

"Your pelo wants cutting," dijo el Hatter. He had been looking at Alicia for some tiempo with great curiosity, y este was su primer speech.

"You should learn not to make personal remarcas," Alicia dijo with some severity; "it's muy rude."

El Hatter opened sus ojos muy wide on hearing this; pero all he *dijo* was, "Why es un cuervo like a writing-desk?"

"Come, we shall have some fun now!" pensó Alicia. "Me alegra que they've begun asking riddles.—Yo creo que I can guess that," ella agregó aloud.

"Do you mean que you think you can find out the answer to it?" dijo la March Hare.

"Exactly so," dijo Alicia.

"Then you should say what you mean," la March Hare went on.

"I do," Alicia hastily replicó; "at least—al menos I mean lo que digo—that's the same cosa, you know."

"Not the same cosa a bit!" dijo el Hatter. "You might just igualmente say que 'I see what I eat' is the same cosa as 'I eat what I see'!"

"You might just igualmente say," added la March Hare, "que 'I like what I get' is the same cosa as 'I get what I like'!"

"You might just igualmente say," added el Dormratón, who seemed to be talking in his sleep, "that 'I breathe when I sleep' is the same cosa as 'I sleep when I breathe'!"

"It *is* the same cosa with you," dijo el Hatter, y aquí la conversación droppeó, y el grupo sateó silencioso for un minuto, mientras Alicia pensó que over all ella podia remembrear about cuernos y writing-desks, which wasn't mucho.

El Hatter was the first to break the silence. "What día of the month is it?" él dijo, turning to Alicia: he had taken his watch out of his pocket, y estaba looking at it uneasily, shaking it every now y then, y holding it to his ear.

Alicia considered un poquito, y entonces dijo "The fourth."

"Two days wrong!" sighed el Hatter. "I told you mantequilla wouldn't suit the works!" he added looking angrily at la March Hare.

"It was the *best* mantequilla," la March Hare meekly replicó.

"Yes, pero algunos crumbs must have got in también," el Hatter grumbled: "you shouldn't have put it in with the bread-knife."

La March Hare took the watch y looked at it gloomily: then he dipped it into his cup of tea, y looked at it otra vez: pero he could pensar of nada better to say than his first remarca, "It was the *best* mantequilla, tú sabes."

Alicia had been looking over sus hombros con some curiosity. "What a funny watch!" she remarcó. "It tells el día del month, y doesn't tell qué o'clock es!"

"Why should it?" muttered el Hatter. "Does *your* watch tell you what year it is?"

"Of course not," Alicia replicó muy readily: "pero that's because it stays the same year for such a long tiempo together."

"Which is just the case with *mine*," dijo el Hatter.

Alicia se sintió dreadfully puzzled. El Hatter's remarca seemed to have no sort of meaning in it, y sin embargo it was certainly English. "I don't quite understand you," ella dijo, tan politeamente as she could.

"El Dormratón está asleep otra vez," dijo el Hatter, y él poureó a little hot tea upon su nose.

El Dromratón shook su cabeza impatiently, y dijo, without opening sus ojos, "Of course, of course; just what I was going to remarcar myself."

"Have you guessed the riddle yet?" el Hatter dijo, turning to Alicia otra vez.

"No, I give it up," Alicia replicó: "what's la respuesta?"

"I haven't the slightest idea," dijo el Hatter.

"Ni yo," dijo la March Hare.

Alicia sighed weareamente. "Yo pienso you might do algo better con el tiempo," ella dijo, "than waste it en preguntar riddles que no tienen respuesta."

"If you knew Time tan bien como I do," dijo el Hatter, "you wouldn't talk about wasting *it*. It's *him*."

"I don't know what you mean," dijo Alicia.

"Of course you don't!" el Hatter dijo, tossing su cabeza contemptuously. "I dare say you never even spoke to Time!"

"Perhaps not," Alicia cautiousamente replicó: "pero I know I have to beat time when I learn music."

"Ah! that accounts for it," dijo el Hatter. "He wo'n't stand beating. Now, if you only kept on good terms with him, he'd do casi cualquier cosa you liked with el reloj. For instance, suppose it were nine o'clock in the morning, just time to begin lecciones: you'd solamente have to whisper a hint to Time, y round goes el reloj in a twinkling! Half-past one, time for dinner!"

("Yo only wish it was," la March Hare dijo to itself con un whisper.)

"That would be grand, certainly," dijo Alicia thoughtfully: "pero then—I shouldn't be hungry for it, tú sabes."

"Not at first, perhaps," dijo el Hatter: "pero you could keep it to half-past one as long as you liked."

"Is that el way *you* manage?" Alicia preguntó.

El Hatter shook su cabeza mournamente. "Not I!" él replicó. "We quarrelled last Marzo—just before *he* went loco, tú sabes—" (pointing with his tea spoon la March Hare,) "—it was at the great concierto given by la Reina de Corazones, y I had to cantar

> *'Twinkle, twinkle, little bat!*
> *Como I wonder qué you're at!'*

Tú sabes la canción, perhaps?"

"I've heard algo like it," dijo Alicia.

"It goes on, tú sabes," el Hatter continuó, "in this way:—

> *'Up arriba el world you fly,*
> *Como un tea-tray en el sky.*
> *Twinkle, twinkle—'"*

Aquí el Dormratón shook itself, y began cantando en su sleep "*Twinkle, twinkle, twinkle, twinkle—*" y went on so long que they had to pinchearlo to make it stop.

"Bien, I'd hardly finishear el primer verso," dijo el Hatter, "when la Reina jumpeó y bawled out, 'He's murdering el tiempo! Off con su cabeza!'"

"How dreadfully salvaje!" exclamó Alicia.

"Y ever since that," el Hatter went on in a mournful tono, "he wo'n't do a cosa I ask! It's always six o'clock now."

A bright idea came into Alicia's cabeza. "Is that the reason so muchas tea-things are put out here?" she asked.

"Yes, that's it," dijo el Hatter with a sigh: "it's always tea-time, y we've no tiempo pa'washer las cosas between whiles."

"Then you keep moving round, I suppose?" dijo Alicia.

"Exactly so," dijo el Hatter: "as las cosas get used up."

"Pero what happens when you come to the beginning otra vez?" Alicia ventured to ask.

"Suppose we cambiamos el sujecto," la March Hare interrumpió, yawning. "I'm getting tired de esto. I vote the young lady tells us un cuento."

"I'm afraid I don't know one," dijo Alicia, muy alarmada at the proposal.

"Entonces el Dormratón shall!" they both cried. "Wake up, Dormratón!" Y ellos pinchearon it on both sides al mismo tiempo.

El Dormratón slowly abrió sus ojos. "I wasn't asleep," él dijo in a hoarse, feeble voz: "I heard every word you fellows were saying."

"Tell us a story!" dijo la March Hare.

"Yes, por favor, do!" pleadeó Alicia.

"Y debe ser quick about it," added the Hatter, "or tú vas a estar asleep otra vez before it's done."

"Había una vez tres little hermanitas," el Dormratón empezó en una great hurry; "y sus nombres eran Elese, Laicia y Tili; y ellas vivían en el bottom de un pozo—"

"What did they live on?" dijo Alicia, who always took un great interés en cuestiones of eating y drinqueando.

"They lived on treacle," dijo el Dormratón, after thinking un minuto or two.

"They couldn't have done that, tú sabes," Alicia gently remarcó; "they'd have been enfermos."

"So they were," dijo el Dormratón; "*muy* enfermos."

Alicia tried to fancy pa'sí misma what such an extraordinary ways of living would be like, pero it puzzled her too much, so she went on: "Pero why did they live at the bottom de un pozo?"

"Take some more tea," la March Hare le dijo a Alicia, muy earnestamente.

"I've had nada yet," Alicia replicó en un offended tono, "so I can't take más."

"You mean you can't take *less*," dijo el Hatter: "it's very easy to take *more* than nada."

"Nobody asked *your* opinion," dijo Alicia.

"Who's making personal remarcas now?" el Hatter asked triumphantly.

Alicia did not quite know what to say to this: so she helped herself to some tea y pan-y-mantequilla, y luego turned to el Dormratón, y repeated su cuestión. "Why did they live at the bottom de un pozo?"

El Dormratón otra vez took un minuto or two to pensar about it, y luego dijo, "Busca un treacle-pozo."

"No hay such cosa!" Alicia was beginning muy angrily, pero el Hatter y la March Hare went "Sh! sh!" y el Dormratón sulkily remarcó, "If you can't be civil, you'd better finish the story for yourself."

"No, por favor go on!" Alicia dijo muy humblemente; "I wo'n't interrupt otra vez. I dare say there may be *one*."

"One, indeed!" dijo el Dormratón indignadamente. Pero, he consented to go on. "Entonces estas tres little hermanitas—they were learning to draw, tú sabes—"

"What did they draw?" dijo Alicia, quite forgeteando her promesa.

"Treacle," dijo el Dormratón, without considering at all this tiempo.

"I want a clean cup," interrupted the Hatter: "let's all move one place on."

He moved on as he spoke, y el Dormratón followed him: la March Hare se mudó al Dormratón's lugar, y Alicia algo unwillingly took the place de la March Hare. The Hatter was the only one who got any ventaja from the cambio: y Alicia estaba a good deal peor que before, as la March Hare had just upset the milk-jug into his plato.

Alicia did not wish a ofender al Dormratón otra vez, so she began muy cautiously: "Pero I don't understand. Where did they draw the treacle from?"

"You can draw water out de un water-pozo," dijo el Hatter; "so I should think you could draw treacle out de un treacle-pozo—eh, estúpida?"

"Pero they were *in* el pozo," Alicia dijo al Dormratón, not choosing to notice this last remarca.

"Of course they were," dijo el Dormratón; "—bastante in."

Esta respuesta so confused a la pobre Alicia, que she let el Dormratón go on por some tiempo sin interrupting it.

"They were learning to draw," el Dormratón went on, yawning y rubbing sus ojos, for it was getting muy sleepy; "y ellos drew all manner of cosas—todo lo que empieza con una M—"

"Por qué con una M?" dijo Alicia.

"Por qué no?" dijo la March Hare.

Alicia estaba silente.

El Dormratón had closed sus ojos by this tiempo, y was going off into a doze; pero, on being pincheada by el Hatter, it woke up otra vez con un mini shriek, y went on: "—que empieza con una M, such as los mouse-trampas, y la moon, y la memoria, and muchamente—tú sabes: tú dices algo tiene 'mucho de muchamente'—did you ever see such a cosa como un drawing de un muchamente?"

"De veras, now you me preguntas," dijo Alicia, very muy confused, "Yo don't think—"

"Then tú shouldn't hablar," dijo el Hatter.

This pedazo of rudeness was more than Alicia could soportar: she got up in great disgust, y walked off; el Dormratón fell asleep instantly, y neither of the others took the least notice of her going, though she looked back once or twice, half hoping que they would call after her: el last tiempo she saw them, they were trying to put el Dormratón dentro del teapot.

"At any rate I'll never go *there* otra vez!" dijo Alicia as she picked her way through the wood. "It's la más estúpida tea-party I ever was at en toda vida!"

Justo mientras ella decía esto, she noticed que one of los árboles tenia una peurta leadeando right into it. "Eso es muy curioso!" ella pensó. "Pero todo es curioso hoy. Yo pienso I may igualmente go in at once." And ella se fue.

Otra vez she found herself in the long hall, y cerca to la pequeña glass mesa. "Now, I'll manage better this tiempo," ella dijo pa'sí misma, y began by taking la little golden llavecita, y unloqueó la puerta que ledeaba into el jardín. Then she went to work nibbling at the mushroom (she had kept un pedazo of it en su bolsillo) till she was about a foot high: then she walked down el little pasajito: y *then*—she found herself at last en el beautiful jardín, among the bright flower-beds y las cool fountains.

El Croque-Piso de la Reina

Un large rose-tree stood cerca de la entrance del jardín: las rosas growing on it were white, pero there were tres jardineros at it, busily painting them red. Alicia pensó this una muy curious cosa, y ella went nearer a verlos, y just as she came up to them she heard one of them say, "Look out now, Five! Don't go splashing paint over me like that!"

"I couldn't help it," dijo Five, in a sulky tono; "Seven jogged my elbow."

On which Seven looked up y dijo, "That's right, Five! Always lay the blame on others!"

"*You'd* better not talk!" dijo Five. "I heard la Reina say only yesterday you deserved to be beheaded!"

"What for?" dijo the one who had spoken first.

"That's none of *your* business, Two!" dijo Seven.

"Yes, it *is* his business!" dijo Five, "y I'll tell him—it was por traer al cocinero tulip-roots instead of cebollas."

Seven flung down his brush, y acababan de decir "Bueno, of all the unjust cosas—" when su ojo chanceó to fall upon Alicia, as she stood watching them, y he checked himself suddenly: the others looked round also, y all of them bowed low.

"Would you tell me," dijo Alicia, a little timidamente, "why you are painting those roses?"

Five y Seven dijeron nada, pero looked at Two. Two began in a low voice, "Why el facto is, you see, Miss, this here ought to have been a *red* rose-tree, y we put una white one por error; and if la Reina was to find it out, we should all have nuestras cabezas cut off, tú sabes. So you see, Miss, we're doing our best, afore she comes, to—" En ese momento Five, que estaba anciosamente looking across el jardín, called out "La Reina! La Reina!" y los tres jardineros instantaneamente threw themselves plano upon sus caras. There was a sound of muchos footsteps, y Alicia looked round, eager to ver la Reina.

First came ten soldiers carrying clubs; these were all shaped like los tres jardineros, oblong y flat, with sus manos y pies at the corners: next los diez courtiers; these were ornamented all over con diamantes, y walked two y two, as the soldiers did. After these came the royal niños; there were diez de ellos, y los little dears came jumpeando merrily along mano a mano, in couples: they were all ornamentados with corazones. Next came the guests, mostly Reyes y Reinas, y among them Alicia recognised el Rabit Blanco: it was talking in a hurried nervous manner, smiling a todo que was said, y went by without noticing her. Then followed el Knave de Corazones, carrying el Rey's crown on a crimson velvet cojín; y, last of all this grand procesión, venían *el Rey y la Reina de Corazones*.

Alicia estaba algo doubtful whether she ought not to lie down on su cara like los tres jardineros, pero ella no podia remembrear ever having heard of such a regla at procesiones; "and besides, what would be the use of una procesión," pensó ella, "if people had all to lie down upon sus caras, so that they couldn't see it?" So she stood still where she was, y waited.

When la procesión came opposite to Alicia, they all stopped y looked at her, y la Reina dijo severemente "Who is this?" Ella se lo dijo al Knave de Corazones, who only bowed y smiled in reply.

"Idiota!" dijo la Reina, tossing her cabeza impaciente-mente; y, turning to Alicia, she went on, "What's your name, child?"

"My name es Alicia, so por favor your Majesty," dijo Alicia muy politely; pero she added, pa'sí misma, "Why, they're only un pack de cartas, after all. I needn't be afraid of them!"

"Y who are *these*?" dijo la Reina, pointing a los tres jardineros who were lying round the rosetree; for, you see, mientras ellos were lying en sus caras, y el pattern de sus backs era el same as the rest del pack, ella could not decir whether they eran jardineros, or soldados, or courtiers, or tres de sus own children.

"How should I know?" dijo Alicia, surprised at her own coraje. "It's no business of *mine*."

La Reina se turneó crimson with fury, y, after glaring at her for a momento like a wild beast, screamed "Off con su cabeza! Off—"

"Tonterías!" dijo Alicia, muy loudly y decididamente, y la Reina estaba silente.

El Rey laid su mano upon her brazo, y timidamente dijo "Consider, my dear: she is only a child!"

La Reina turneó angrily away de él, y dijo al Knave: "Turn them over!"

El Knave did so, muy carefully, with one foot.

"Get up!" dijo la Reina, in a shrill, loud voice, y los tres jardineros instantly jumped up, y began bowing to el Rey, la Reina, los royal niños, y todos los demás.

"Leave off that!" screameó la Reina. "You make me giddy." Y then, turning to the rose-tree, she went on, "What *have* you been doing here?"

"May it satisfacer a su Majesty," dijo Two, en un muy humblemente tono, going down on one knee as he spoke, "we were trying—"

"I see!" dijo la Reina, who had meanwhile been examining the roses. "Off con sus cabezas!" y la procesión moved on, tres de los soldados remaining behind to execute los unfortunate jardineros, who ran to Alicia for protección.

"You sha'n't be beheaded!" dijo Alicia, y ella put them into a large flower-pot que stood near. The three soldiers wandered about por un minuto or two, looking for them, y then quietly marched off after the others.

"Are their cabezas off?" shouteó la Reina.

"Their cabezas are gone, if it satisface a su Majesty!" the soldiers shouted in reply.

"That's right!" shouteó la Reina. "Can you play croqueta?"

Los soldados were silentes, y looked at Alicia, as la cuestión was evidentemente meant for her.

"Yes!" shouteó Alicia.

"Come on, then!" roareó la Reina, y Alicia joined la procesión, wondering very mucho what would happen next.

"It's—it's a muy fine día!" dijo una timid voz at her side. She was walking by el Rabit Blanco, who was peeping anciosamente into su cara.

"Very," dijo Alicia: "—where's la Duquesa?"

"Hush! Hush!" dijo el Rabit en un low, hurriado tono. He looked anciosamente over his hombro as he spoke, y then raised himself upon tiptoe, put his mouth close to her ear, y whispereó "She's under sentence of execución."

"What for?" dijo Alicia.

"Did you say 'What a pity!'?" el Rabit preguntó.

"No, I didn't," dijo Alicia: "I don't pienso it's at all a pity. To dije 'What for?'"

"She boxed la Reina's prejas—" el Rabit empezó. Alicia gave un mini scream of laughter. "Oh, hush!" el Rabit whispered in a frightened tono. "La Reina will hearear you! You see, she came algo late, y la Reina dijo—"

"Get to your places!" shouteó la Reina en una voz de thunder, y people empezaron a runnar about en todas direcciones, tumbling up against each other; pero, they got settled down in un minuto or two, y el juego began. Alicia pensó que ella had never seen such a curious croqueta-ground en su vida; todo era ridges y furrows; las balls eran live hedgehogs, los mallets live flamingoes, y los soldiers had to double themselves up y to stand en sus manos y pies, to make los arcos.

La chief dificultad Alicia found at first era en managear her flamingo: ella succeeded en getting su cuerpo tucked away, comfortablemente enough, under su brazo, with its legs hanging down, pero generally, just as she had got its neck nicely straightened out, y was going a darle al hedgehog un blow con su cabeza, it *would* twist itself round y look up en su cara, with such a puzzled expresión que ella could not help a burstear out riendo: y when she had got su cabeza down, y was going to begin otra vez, it was muy provoking to find que el hedgehog had unrolled itself, y estaba en el acto de crawleando away: besides all this, there was generally a ridge or furrow in the way wherever she wanted to send the hedgehog to, y, as the doubled-up soldiers were always getting up y walking off to other parts of the ground, Alicia soon came to la conclusión que it was un juego muy difícil indeed.

Los players todos played at once without waiting sus turnos, quarreleando all the while, y fighteando por los hedgehogs; y en un muy short tiempo la Reina was in una furious pasión, y went stampeando about, y shouteando "Off con su cabeza!" about once en un minuto.

Alicia began to feel muy uneasy: to be sure, she had not as yet had any dispute con la Reina, pero she knew que it might happen any minuto, "y then," pensó she, "what would become of me? They're dreadfully fond of beheading people here; the great wonder is, that there's any one left alive!"

She was looking about for some way of escape, y wondering whether she could get away without being seen, when she noticed a curious appearance in the air: it puzzled her very mucho at first, pero, after watching it un minuto or two, she made it out to be a grin, y ella dijo pa'sí misma "Es el Gato de Cheshire: now I shall have somebody to talk to."

"How are you getting on?" dijo el Gato, as soon as there was mouth enough for it to speak with.

Alicia esperó till los ojos appeared, y luego nodded. "It's no use speaking to it," she pensó, "till its ears have come, o por lo menos one of them." In another minuto the whole cabeza appeared, y luego Alicia put down her flamingo, y empezó una account del juego, feeling muy contenta she had someone to listen to her. El Gato parecía pensar que there was enough of it now in sight, y no more of it appeared.

"I don't pienso they play at all fairly," Alicia empezó, in algo de un complaining tono, "y they all quarrel so dreadfully one can't hear oneself speak—y they don't seem to have any reglas en particular; al menos, if there are, nadie attends a ellos—y you've no idea how confuso it is all las cosas que estaban vivas; for instance, there's the arch I've got to go through next walking about at the other end of the ground— y I should have croqueteado la Reina's hedgehog just ahora, only it ran away when it saw mine coming!"

"Cómo te gusta la Reina?" dijo el Gato en una low voz.

"Not at all," dijo Alicia: "she's so extremely—" Just then she noticed que la Reina was close behind her, listening: so she went on, "—likely to win, that it's hardly worth while finishing el juego."

La Reina smileó y passed on.

"Who *are* you talking to?" dijo el Rey, going up to Alicia, y looking at el Gato's cabeza con gran curiosidad.

"It's an amigo of mine—al Gato de Cheshire," dijo Alicia: "allow me to introduce it."

"I don't like the look of it at all," dijo el Rey: "pero, it may kiss mi mano if it likes."

"I'd prefiero not," el Gato remarcó.

"Don't be impertinente," dijo el Rey, "y don't look at me like that!" He got behind Alicia as he spoke.

"Un gato puede parecer un rey," dijo Alicia. "I've read that in some book, pero no me remembreo dónde."

"Bueno, it must be removeado," dijo el Rey muy decidedamente, y he called la Reina, who was passeando at el momento, "My dear! I wish you would have este gato removeado!"

La Reina tenía solamente un way of settling todas las dificultades, grandes or small. "Off con su cabeza!" ella dijo, without even looking alrededor.

"I'll fetch the execucionador myself," dijo el Rey eagermente, y él se hurrieó off.

Alicia pensó she might igualmente go back, y see how el juego was going on, as she heard la Reina's voz in the distance, screaming con pasión. She had already heard her sentence three of the players to be executed for having missed their turns, y ella did not like el look de las cosas at all, as el juego was in such confusión que she never knew whether it was her turn or not. So she went in search of her hedgehog.

El hedgehog was engaged in una lucha with another hedgehog, which seemed to Alicia an excellent opportunity for croqueting one of them with the other: la única dificultad was, que her flamingo was gone across to the other side of el jardín, where Alicia could see it trying in a helpless sort of way to fly up into a tree.

By el tiempo she had caught the flamingo y brought it back, the fight was over, y both the hedgehogs were out of sight: "pero it doesn't matter mucho," pensó Alicia, "as all the arches are gone from this side of the ground." So she tucked it away debajo de su brazo, que it might not escaparse otra vez, y went back por un poquito más de conversación con su friend.

When she got back to el Gato de Cheshire, she was surprised to find quite a large crowd collected round it: there was a dispute going on between the execucionador, el Rey, y la Reina, who were all talking at once, while all the rest were quite silent, y looked muy uncomfortable.

El momento que Alicia appeared, she was appealed to by all three to settle la cuestión, y they repeated their argumentos to her, though, as they all spoke at once, she found it muy difícil indeed to make out exactamente lo que ellos dijeron.

El execucionador's argumento was, que you couldn't cut off una cabeza unless there was a body to cut it off from: que he had never had to hacer such a cosa before, y él wasn't going to begin at *his* tiempo of la vida.

El Rey's argumento was, que algo that had una cabeza could be beheaded, y que you weren't to hablar tonterías.

La Reina's argumento era, que if algo wasn't done about it en menos de no tiempo she'd have everybody execucionado, all round. (It was this last remarca that had made todo el grupo look so grave y ancioso.)

Alicia could pensar of nada else to say pero "It belongs to la Duquesa: you'd better ask *her* about it."

"She's in prisión," la Reina dijo al executionador: "fetch her here." Y the executioner went off like an arrow.

El Gato's cabeza began fading away el momento he was gone, y, by the tiempo he had come back with la Duquesa, it had entirely disappeared; so el Rey y el executioner ran wildly up y down looking for it, while el resto del grupo went back to el juego.

La Story de la Mock Tortuga

"You can't pensar how contenta I am to see you otra vez, you dear old cosa!" dijo la Duquesa, as she tucked su brazo afeccionalmente into Alicia's, y they walked off together.

Alicia was muy contenta to find her in such a pleasant temper, y pensó pa'sí misma que perhaps it was only the pepper que had made her so salvaje when they met en la cocina.

"When *I'm* una Duquesa," ella dijo pa'sí misma, (not en un muy hopeful tono though), "I wo'n't have any pepper in my kitchen *at all*. Soup does muy bien without—Maybe it's always pimienta que makes people hot-tempered," she continuó, very mucho pleasedo at having encontrado un new kind of regla, "y vinagre que makes them sour—y camomila que makes them bitter—y—y barley-sugar y such cosas that make niños sweet-tempered. I only wish la gente knew that: then they wouldn't be so stingy about it, tú sabes—"

She had quite olvidado la Duquesa by this tiempo, y was un poquito startled when ella heard su voice close to su oído. "You're pensando about algo, my dear, y that makes you forgetear to talk. I can't tell you just ahora what the moral of that is, pero voy a remembrearlo in a bit."

"Perhaps it hasn't one," Alicia ventured to remarcar.

"Tut, tut, child!" dijo la Duquesa. "Todo's got a moral, if only you can find it." Y ella squeezeó herself up más cerca de Alicia's side as ella spoke.

Alicia did not mucho like keeping so close to her: first, porque la Duquesa estaba *muy* ugly; y secondly, porque she was exactly the right height to rest her chin upon Alicia's hombro, y it was an uncomfortablemene sharp chin. Pero, she did not like ser ruda, so she bore it tan bien as she pudo.

"El juego's going on algo better ahora," ella dijo, by way of keeping up the conversación un poquito.

"'Tis so," dijo la Duquesa: "y the moral of that is—'Oh, 'tis love, 'tis love, que makes the world go round!'"

"Somebody dijo," Alicia whispered, "that it's done by everybody minding their own business!"

"Ah, bueno! It means mucho the same cosa," dijo la Duquesa, digging su sharp mini chin into Alicia's hombro mientras she added, "y the moral of *that* is—'Take care of the sense, y the sounds will take care of themselves'."

"How fond she is of finding morals en cosas!" Alicia pensó pa'sí misma.

"I dare say you're wondering why I don't put mi brazo round tu cintura," la Duquesa dijo después de una pausa: "the reason is, que I'm doubtful about the temper of your flamingo. Shall I try the experiment?"

"*He* might bite," Alicia cautiously replicó, not feeling at all anciosa to have the experiment tried.

"Muy true," dijo la Duquesa: "flamingoes y mustard both bite. Y the moral of that is—'Pájaros of a feather flock together'."

"Only mustard isn't a pájaro," Alicia remarcó.

"Right, as usual," dijo la Duquesa: "what a clear way you have of putting cosas!"

"It's un mineral, yo *pienso*," dijo Alicia.

"Of course it is," dijo la Duquesa, who seemed ready to agree to todo lo que dijo Alicia; "there's a large mustard-mine near here. Y the moral of that is—'The more there is of mine, the less there is of yours'."

"Oh, I know!" exclaimed Alicia, who had not attended to this last remarca, "it's a vegetable. It doesn't look like one, pero it is."

"I quite agree with you," dijo la Duquesa; "y the moral of that is—'Be what you would seem to be'—or if you'd like it put more simply—'Never imagine yourself not to be otherwise than what it might appear to others que what you were or might have been was not otherwise than what you had been would have appeared to them to be otherwise'."

"Yo pienso I should understand that better," Alicia dijo muy politely, "if I had it written down: pero I can't quite follow it as you say it."

"That's nada to what I could say if I chose," la Duquesa replicó, in a pleasedo tono.

"Pray don't trouble yourself to say it any longer than that," dijo Alicia.

"Oh, don't talk about trouble!" dijo la Duquesa. "I make you a present of todo I've said as yet."

"A cheap sort of present!" pensó Alicia. "I'm contenta they don't give birthday regalos like that!" Pero she did not venture to say it out loud.

"Thinking otra vez?" la Duquesa preguntó, with another dig of her sharp mini chin.

"I've a right to think," dijo Alicia sharply, for she was beginning to feel un poquito worried.

"Just about as mucho right," dijo la Duquesa, "as pigs have to fly; y the m—"

Pero here, to Alicia's great sorpresa, la Duquesa's voz died away, even in the middle of her favourite word "moral", y el brazo que was linked into hers began to temblar. Alicia looked up, y there stood la Reina in front of them, with sus brazos foldeados, frowning como una thunderstorm.

"A fine día, su Majestad!" la Duquesa empezó en una low, weak voz.

"Ahora, I give you fair warning," shouteó la Reina, stamping on the ground as she spoke; "either you or your cabeza must be off, y that in about half no tiempo! Take your choice!"

La Duquesa took her choice, y was gone en un momento.

"Let's go on with el juego," la Reina dijo a Alicia; y Alicia was too mucho frightened to say a word, pero slowly followed her back to el croqueta-ground.

Las otras visitas had tomado ventaja de las Reina's absence, y were resting in the shade: pero, el momento they saw her, they hurried back to el juego, la Reina meramente remarcando that a momento's delay would cost them their lives.

All the tiempo they were playing la Reina never left off quarrelling with the other players, y shouting "Off con su cabeza!" Those whom she sentenced were taken into custody by the soldiers, who of course had to leave off being arches to do this, so que by the end of half an hour or so there were no arches left, y all the players, except el Rey, la Reina, y Alicia, were in custody y under sentence of execución.

Entonces la Reina left off, quite out of breath, y le dijo a Alicia, "Have you seen la Mock Tortuga yet?"

"No," dijo Alicia. "I don't even know what a Mock Tortuga is."

"It's la cosa que la Mock Tortuga Soup es made de," dijo la Reina.

"I never saw one, or heard of one," dijo Alicia.

"Come on, then," dijo la Reina, "y he shall tell you his history,"

As they walked off together, Alicia heard el Rey decir en una low voz, to the company generally, "You are all pardoned."

"Come, *That's* a good cosa!" ella dijo pa'sí misma, for she had felt quite unhappy at the number of execuciones la Reina had ordered.

Ellos muy soon came upon un Gryfón, lying fast asleep in the sun. (*If* you don't know what a Gryfón is, mira la picture.) "Up, lazy cosa!" dijo la Reina, "y take this young lady to see la Mock Tortuga, y to hear his history. I must go back y see after some execuciones I have ordered"; y ella walked off, leaving Alicia alone with el Gryfón. Alicia did not quite like the look of the creature, pero on the whole she pensó it would be quite tant seguro to stay con él as to go after esa salvaje Reina: so she waited.

El Gryfón sat up y rubbed sus ojos: then it watched la Reina till she was out of sight: then it chuckled. "What fun!" dijo el Gryfón, half to itself, half to Alicia.

"What *is* the fun?" dijo Alicia.

"Why, *she*," dijo el Gryfón. "It's all her fancy, that: they never execute a nadie, tú sabes. Come on!"

"Everybody says 'come on!' here," pensó Alicia, as she went slowly after it: "I never was so ordered about en toda mi vida, never!"

They had not gone far before they saw la Mock Tortuga in the distance, sitting sad y lonely en un ledge pequeñito de roca, y, as they came más cerca, Alicia could oir him sighing as if su corazón se fuera a romper. She pitied him deeply. "What is his sorrow?" she asked el Gryfón, y el Gryfón respondió, muy nearly en las mismas palabras as before, "It's all his fancy, that: he hasn't got no sorrow, tú sabes. Come on!"

So they went up to la Mock Tortuga, who looked at them with large ojos full of lágrimas, pero dijo nada.

"This here young lady," dijo el Gryfón, "she wants for to know your history, she do."

"I'll tell it her," dijo la Mock Tortuga in a deep, hollow tono: "sit down, both of you, y don't speak a word till I've finished."

So ellos sat down, y nobody spoke por some minutos. Alicia pensó pa'sí misma, "I don't see how he can *even* finish, if he doesn't begin." Pero she waited patiently.

"Once," dijo la Mock Tortuga at last, with a deep sigh, "I was a real Turtle."

Esas palabras were followed por un muy long silence, broken only by an occasional exclamación of "Hjckrrh!" del Gryfón, y el constant heavy sobbing of la Mock Tortuga. Alicia estaba muy nearly getting up y saying, "Gracias, señor, por su interesting cuento," pero she could not help pensando there *must* be more to come, so she sat still y dijo nada.

"Cuando éramos little," la Mock Tortuga went on at last, more calmly, though still sobbing un poquito now y then, "we went to school in the sea. The master was an old Turtle—we used to call him Tortoise—"

"Why did you call him Tortoise, if he wasn't one?" Alicia asked.

"We called him Tortoise porque he taught us," dijo la Mock Tortuga angrily: "de veras you are muy dull!"

"You ought to be ashamed of yourself for asking such a simple cuestión," agregó el Gryfón; y then they both sat silent y miraron a la pobre Alicia, who felt ready to sink into la tierra. At last el Gryfón dijo a la Mock Tortuga, "Drive on, old fellow! Don't be all día about it!" y he went on in these words:

"Yes, we went to school in the sea, though you mayn't believe it—"

"Yo nunca dije I didn't!" interrupted Alicia.

"You did," dijo la Mock Tortuga.

"Hold your lengua!" added el Gryfón, antes que Alicia could speak otra vez. La Mock Tortuga went on.

"We had the best of educaciones—in facto, we went to school every día—"

"*I've* been to a day-school, too," dijo Alicia; "you needn't be so proud as all that."

"With extras?" asked la Mock Tortuga un poquito anciosamente.

"Yes," dijo Alicia, "we learned French y music."

"Y washing?" dijo la Mock Tortuga.

"Certainly not!" dijo Alicia indignantly.

"Ah! then yours wasn't una muy buena school," dijo la Mock Tortuga in a tono of great relief. "Now at *ours* they had at the end of the bill, 'French, music, *y washing*—extra'."

"You couldn't have wanted it mucho," dijo Alicia; "living at the bottom of the sea."

"I couldn't afford to learn it." dijo la Mock Tortuga with a sigh. "I only took the regular course."

"What was that?" inquired Alicia.

"Reeling y Writhing, of course, to begin with," la Mock Tortuga replicó; "y luego las branches difíciles of Arithmetic—Ambición, Distracción, Uglificación, y Derisin."

"Yo nunca heard de 'Uglificación'," Alicia ventured to say. "Qué es eso?"

El Gryfón lifted up both its paws en surpresa. "What! Never heard of uglificar!" it exclaimed. "Tú sabes what to beautify is, I suppose?"

"Yes," dijo Alicia doubtfully: "it means—to—make—cualquier cosa—prettier."

"Bueno, then," el Gryfón went on, "if you don't know what to uglificar is, you *are* a simpleton."

Alicia did not feel encouraged to ask any otras cuestiones about it, so she turned to la Mock Tortuga, y dijo "What else had you to learn?"

"Bueno, there was Mystery," la Mock Tortuga replicó, counting off the sujetos on his flappers, "—Mystery, ancient y modern, with Seaography: then Drawling—el Drawling-master was an old conger-eel, que used to come once a week: *He* taught us Drawling, Stretching, y Fainting en Coils."

"What was *that* like?" dijo Alicia.

"Bueno, I can't show it you myself," la Mock Tortuga dijo: "Soy muy stiff. Y el Gryfón nunca lo aprendió."

"Hadn't tiempo," dijo el Gryfón: "I went to the Classics master, though. Él era un old crab, *él* era."

"I never went a él," la Mock Tortuga dijo with a sigh: "he taught Laughing y Grief, they used to say."

"So he did, so he did," dijo el Gryfón, sigheyo en su turno; y both criaturas hid their caras en sus paws.

"Y how muchas hours al día did you do lecciones?" dijo Alicia, in a hurry to cambiar el sujeto.

"Ten hours the first día," dijo la Mock Tortuga: "nine the next, y so on."

"What a curious plan!" exclaimed Alicia.

"That's the reason they're called lecciones," el Gryfón remarcó: "porque they lessen from día to día."

Esta era quite a new idea to Alicia, y ella pensó it over un poquito antes de que she made her next remarca. "Then the eleventh día must have been un holiday?"

"Of course it was," dijo la Mock Tortuga.

"Y how did you manage on the twelfth?" Alicia went on eagerly.

"That's enough about lecciones," el Gryfón interrupted en un muy decided tono: "tell her algo about los juegos now."

La Cuadrilla del Lobster

La Mock Tortuga sighed deeply, y drew the back of one flapper across sus ojos. He looked at Alicia, y tried to speak, pero por un minuto or two sobs choked his voice. "Same as if he had a bone in his throat," dijo el Gryfón: y it set to work shaking him y punching him in the back. At last la Mock Tortuga recovered his voice, y, with tears running down his cheeks, he went on otra vez:—

"You may not have lived mucho under the sea—" ("I haven't," dijo Alicia) "—y perhaps you were never even introduced to un lobster—" (Alicia began to say "I once tasted—" pero checked herself hastily, y dijo "No, nunca") "—so you can have no idea what a delightful cosa un Lobster Quadrille es!"

"No, indeed," dijo Alicia. "What sort of a dance is it?"

"Why," dijo el Gryfón, "you first form into a line along the sea-shore—"

"Two lines!" cried la Mock Tortuga. "Seals, turtles, salmon, y so on; then, when you've cleared all the jelly-fish out of el camino—"

"*That* generally takes some tiempo," interrupted el Gryfón.

"—you advance twice—"

"Each with un lobster como un partner!" cried el Gryfón.

"Of course," la Mock Tortuga dijo: "advance twice, set to partners—"

"—change lobsters, y retire en el same order," continued el Gryfón.

"Then, tú sabes," la Mock Tortuga went on, "you throw the—"

"Los lobsters!" shouted el Gryfón, with a bound into the air.

"—as far out to sea as you can—"

"Swim after them!" screamed el Gryfón.

"Turn a somersault in the sea!" cried la Mock Tortuga, capering wildly about.

"Change lobster's otra vez!" yelled el Gryfón at the top of its voice.

"Back to tierra otra vez, y that's all the first figure," dijo la Mock Tortuga, suddenly dropping his voice; y las dos criaturas, who had been jumpeando about like cosas locas all this tiempo, sat down otra vez muy sadly y quietly, y looked a Alicia.

"It must be a muy pretty dance," dijo Alicia timidamente.

"Would you like to see un poquito of it?" dijo la Mock Tortuga.

"Very mucho indeed," dijo Alicia.

"Come, let's try the first figure!" dijo la Mock Tortuga al Gryfón. "We can do sin lobsters, tú sabes. Which shall sing?"

"Oh, *you* sing," dijo el Gryfón. "I've forgotten the words."

So they began solemnly dancing round and round Alicia, every now y then treading on her toes when they passed too

close, y waving their forepaws to mark el tiempo, while la
Mock Tortuga cantó esto, muy slowly y tristemente:—

"Will you walk un poco faster?" dijo un whiting a una snail.
"Hay un porpoise close behind us, y he's treading en mi tail.
Ve cómo eagerly los lobsters y las turtles all advance!
Ellos están waiteando en el shingle—will you come y join la
  dance?
  Will you, wo'n't you, will you, wo'n't you, will you join la
    dance?
  Will you, wo'n't you, will you, wo'n't you, wo'n't you join la
    dance?

"You can de veras have no noción cuán delightful it will be
When they take us up y throw us, con los lobsters, out al sea!"
Pero the snail replicó "Too far, too far!" y gave una look
  askance—
Dijo he thanked the whiting kindly, pero he would not join la
  dance.
  Would not, could not, would not, could not, would not join la
    dance.
  Would not, could not, would not, could not, could not join la
    dance.

"What matters qué tan far we go?" his scaly friend replied.
"Hay otro shore, tú sabes, upon el otro side.
Mientras further off de England es más cerca de la France—
Then turn not pale, querida snail, pero come y join la dance.
  Will you, wo'n't you, will you, wo'n't you, will you join la
    dance?
  Will you, wo'n't you, will you, wo'n't you, wo'n't you join la
    dance?"

"Gracias, la dance es muy interesting to watch," dijo Alicia, feeling muy contenta that it was over at last: "y I do so like esa curiosa canción about el whiting!"

"Oh, as to the whiting," dijo la Mock Tortuga, "they— you've seen them, of course?"

"Yes," dijo Alicia, "I've often seen them at dinn—" ella checked herself hastily.

"Yo no sé dónde Dinn may be," dijo la Mock Tortuga, "pero if you've seen them so often, of course tú sabes what they're like."

"I believe so," Alicia replicó thoughtfully. "They have their tails in their mouths—y they're all over crumbs."

"You're wrong about the crumbs," dijo la Mock Tortuga: "crumbs would all wash off in the sea. Pero they *have* their tails in their mouths; y the reason is—" here la Mock Tortuga yawned y shut sus ojos.—"Tell her about the reason y all that," él le dijo al Gryfón.

"La razón es," dijo el Gryfón, "que they *would* go with los lobsters to the dance. So they got thrown out to sea. So they had to fall a long way. So they got their tails fast in their mouths. So they couldn't get them out otra vez. Eso es todo."

"Gracias," dijo Alicia, "it's muy interesante. I never knew so mucho about a whiting before."

"I can tell you more than that, if you like," dijo el Gryfón. "Do you know why it's called a whiting?"

"I never thought about it," dijo Alicia. "Why?"

"*It does the boots y shoes*." el Gryfón replicó muy solemnly.

Alicia was thoroughly puzzled. "Does the boots y shoes!" she repeated in a wondering tono.

"Why, what are *your* shoes done with?" dijo el Gryfón. "I mean, what makes them so shiny?"

Alicia looked down at them, y considered un poquito before she gave su respuesta. "They're acabados con blacking, yo creo."

"Boots y shoes bajo el mar," el Gryfón went on in a deep voice, "are done con un whiting. Now tú sabes."

"Y qué are they hechos de?" Alicia asked in a tono of great curiosidad.

"Soles and eels, of course," el Gryfón replicó algo impacientemente: "any shrimp could have told you eso."

"If I'd been the whiting," dijo Alicia, whose thoughts were still running on la canción, "I'd have said to the porpoise, 'Keep back, por favor: we don't want *you* with us!'"

"They were obliged to have him with them," la Mock Tortuga dijo: "no wise fish would go anywhere without a porpoise."

"Wouldn't it de veras?" dijo Alicia in a tono of great sorpresa.

"Of course not," dijo la Mock Tortuga: "why, if a fish came to *me*, y told me he was going a journey, I should say 'With what porpoise?'"

"Don't you mean 'purpose'?" dijo Alicia.

"I mean lo que digo," la Mock Tortuga replicó en un offended tono. Y el Gryfón agregó "Come, let's hear some of *your* adventuras."

"I could tell you my adventuras—beginning from esta mañana," dijo Alicia un poco tímidamente: "pero it's no use going back to yesterday, porque yo era entonces una persona diferente."

"Explain all that," dijo la Mock Tortuga.

"No, no! Las adventuras primero," dijo el Gryfón en un tono impaciente: "explanaciones take such a dreadful tiempo."

So Alicia began a contarles sus adventuras from el tiempo cuando ella first saw el Rabit Blanco. She was un poquito nerviosa about it just at first, las dos criaturas got so close to her, one on each side, y opened sus ojos y bocas so *muy* wide, pero she gained coraje as she went on. Sus listeners estaban perfectly callados till she got a la parte about her repeating "*Usté está Viejo, Padre Guillermo*," to el Caterpilar, y las palabras all coming diferentes, y then la Mock Tortuga drew a long breath, y dijo "That's muy curioso."

"It's all about as curious as it can be," dijo el Gryfón.

"It all came diferente!" la Mock Tortuga repeated thoughtfully. "I should like to hear her try y repeat algo nuevo. Tell her to begin." Él miró al Gryfón as if he thought it had some kind of autoridad sobre Alicia.

"Stand up y repite '*Tis la Voz del Sluggard*'," dijo el Gryfón.

"How the critauras order a los demás, y make one repeat lecciones!" pensó Alicia; "I might lo mismo estar en la school at once." Pero, she got up, y began to repeat it, pero su cabeza was so full de los Lobster Quadrille, que she hardly sabía what she was saying, y the words came very extraño indeed:—

"'Tis la voz del Lobster; yo lo oí him declare,
'You have baked me muy brown, I must sugar mi hair.'
As a pato with pestañas, so he con su nose
Trims his cinturón y his botones, y turns out his toes.
When the sands are all secas, él es gay as a lark,
Y will talk in contemptuous tonos of el Shark,
Pero, when the tide se levanta y sharks are around,
Has un tímido y tremulous sound."

"That's diferente from what I used to say when I was a child," dijo el Gryfón.

"Bueno, I never heard it before," dijo la Mock Tortuga; "pero it sounds como una uncommon tontería."

Alicia no dijo nada; she had sat down with her cara en sus manos, wondering if algo would *ever* happen en un natural way otra vez.

"I should like to have it explained," dijo la Mock Tortuga.

"She can't explain it," dijo el Gryfón hastiamente. "Go on with the next verse."

"Pero about his toes?" la Mock Tortuga persisted. "How *could* he turn them out with his nose, tú sabes?"

"Es la first posición en danza," Alicia dijo; pero was dreadfully puzzled by the whole cosa, y longed to cambiar el sujeto.

"Go on with the next verse," the Gryfón repeated impatiently: "it begins 'I passed by su jardin'."

Alicia did not dare to disobey, though she felt sure it would all come wrong, y ella went on en una voz trembleante:—

"I passed by su jardín, y marked, with un ojo,
How el Búho y la Pantera were sharing a piojo;
La Pantera took un pie-crust, y gravy, y meat,
Mientras que el Búho had el plato as its share p'al treat.
When the pie estaba todo finished, el Búho, en un boon,
Fue kindly permitteadp to pocket la spoon:
While la Pantera received cuchillo y tenedor con un growl,
Y concluded el banquet by ——"

"What *is* the use of repeating all that stuff," la Mock Tortuga interrupted, "if you don't explain it as you go on? It's by far la más confusing cosa I ever heard!"

"Yes, I think you'd better leave off," dijo el Gryfón: y Alicia was only too contenta to do so.

"Shall we try another figure del Lobster Quadrille?" el Gryfón went on. "Or would you like la Mock Tortuga to sing you una canción?"

"Oh, una canción, por favor, if la Mock Tortuga would be so kind," Alicia replicó, so eagerly que el Gryfón dijo, in an algo offended tono, "Hm! No accounting for gustos! Sing her 'Turtle Soup,' will you, old fellow?"

La Mock Tortuga sighed deeply, y empezó, en una voz sometimes choked con sobs, a cantar esto:—

"Beautiful Sopa, so rica and green,
Waiting in a hot tureen!
Quién for such dainties would not slopa?
Sopa de la noche, beautiful Sopa!
Sopa de la noche, beautiful Sopa!
    Beau—ootiful Soo—opa!
    Beau—ootiful Soo—opa!
Soo—opa of the e—e—evening,
    Beautiful, beautiful Sopa!

"Beautiful Sopa! Who cares for fish,
Game, or any otro dish?
Quién would not give all else por una
troca solo de beautiful Sopa?
Pennyworth only de beautiful Sopa?
    Beau—ootiful Soo—opa!
    Beau—ootiful Soo—opa!
Soo—opa of the e—e—evening,
    Beautiful, beauti—FUL SOPA!"

"Coro otra vez!" gritó el Gryfón, y la Mock Tortuga had just begun to repeat it, when a cry of "The trial's beginning!" was heard in the distance.

"Come on!" gritó el Gryfón, y, taking Alicia de la mano, it hurried off, without waiting for el final de la canción.

"What trial is it?" Alicia panted as she ran; pero el Gryfón only answered "Come on!" y ran the faster, while more y more faintly came, carried on the breeze que followed them, the melancholy words:—

> *"Soo—oopa of the e—e—evening,*
> *Beautiful, beautiful Sopa!"*

Quién se Robó las Tartas?

El Rey y la Reina de Corazones were seated on their throne when they arrived, with a great crowd assembled about them—all sorts of pequeños pajaritos y bestias, igual que el whole pack de cards: el Knave was standing before them, in chains, with a soldier on each side to guard him; y near el Rey was el Rabit Blanco, with a trumpet en una mano, y a scroll of parchment in the other. En el muy middle de la corte había una mesa, con un large plato de tortas upon it: they looked so good, que it made Alicia muy hungry to look at them—"I wish they'd get the trial done," she pensó, "y hand round the refreshments!" Pero there seemed to be no chance of esto, so she began looking at todo about ella, to pass away el tiempo.

Alicia had never been in a corte of justice before, pero she had read about them in books, y ella was muy contenta to find que she knew the name of casi todo there. "That's the judge," ella dijo pa'sí misma, "because of his great wig."

El judge, by the way, was el Rey; y as he wore his crown over the wig, (look at the frontispiece if you want to see how he did it,) he did not look at all comfortable, y it was certainly not becoming.

"Y that's la jury-box," pensó Alicia, "y those doce criaturas," (she was obliged to say "criaturas", you see, porque some of them were animales, y otros eran pájaros,) "I suppose they are the jurors." Ella dijo esta última palabra two or three veces over pa'sí misma, being algo proud of it: for she pensó, y rightly too, que very pocas little niñitas of her edad conocían el meaning of it at all. Pero, "jury-men" would have done just igual.

Los doce jurors were all writing muy busily on slates. "What are they doing?" Alicia whispered to el Gryfón. "They can't have nada to put down yet, before the trial's begun."

"They're putting down their names," el Gryfón whispered in reply, "for fear they should forgetear them before the end of the trial."

"Cosas estúpidas!" Alicia en unavoz loud, indignante, pero ella stopped hastily, for el Rabit Blanco gritó, "Silencio en la corte!" y el Rey put on sus gafas y looked anciosamente round, to make out who was hablando.

Alicia could ver, igual como si she were miran enciam de sus hombros, que todos los jurors were writing down "cosas estúpidas!" on their slates, y ella could even make out that one of them didn't know how to spell "estúpidas", and que he had to ask his neighbour to tell him. "A nice muddle their slates'll be in before the trial's over!" pensó Alicia.

One of the jurors had a pencil que squeaked. This of course, Alicia could not stand, y ella went round la corte y got behind him, y muy soon found una oportunidad of taking it away. She did it so rápidamente que el pobre mini juror (it was Bill, la Lizard) could not make out at all what had become of it; so, after hunting all about for it, he was obliged to write con un dedo por the rest of el día; y this was of very poquito use, as it left no mark on the slate.

"Herald, read the acusación!" dijo el Rey.

On this el Rabit Blanco blew tres blasts on la trumpeta, y then unrolled the parchment scroll, y read as follows:—

"La Reina de Corazones, she made some tartas,
  Todo en a summer day:
El Knave de Corazones, he stole those tartas,
  Y took them muy away!"

"Consider your verdict," el Rey dijo to el jury.

"Not yet, not yet!" the Rabit hastily interrupted. "There's a great deal to come before that!"

"Call the first witness," dijo el Rey; y el Rabit Blanco blew three blasts on la trumpeta, y called out, "First witness!"

The first witness was el Hatter. He came in with a tea-copa en una mano y un pedazo of pan-y-mantequilla in the other. "I beg pardon, your Majesty," he began, "for bringing these in: pero I hadn't quite finished my tea when I was sent for."

"You ought to have finished," dijo el Rey. "When did you begin?"

El Hatter looked at la March Hare, who had followed him into la corte, brazo-in-brazo with el Dormratón. "Fourteenth of March, I think it was," él dijo.

"Fifteenth," dijo la March Hare.

"Sixteenth," agregó el Dormratón.

"Write that down," el Rey dijo to el jury, y el jury eagerly wrote down all tres dates on their slates, y luego added them up, y reduced la respuesta to shillings y pence.

"Take off your hat," él dijo al Hatter.

"It isn't mine," dijo el Hatter.

"Stolen!" el Rey exclaimed, turning to el jury, who instantly made a memorandum of el facto.

"I keep them to sell," the Hatter added as an explanación; "I've none of my own. I'm a hatter."

Aquí la Reina put on sus gafas, y began staring at el Hatter, who turned pale y fidgeted.

"Give your evidence," dijo el Rey; "y don't be nervous, or I'll have you executed on the spot."

This did not seem to encourage the witness at all: he kept shifting from one foot to the other, looking uneasily a la Reina, y en su confusión he bit a large pedazo out of his tea-copa instead of the pan-y-mantequilla.

Just at this momento Alicia sinitió una muy curious sensación, which puzzled her a good deal until she made out what it was: ella estaba beginning a crecer larger otra vez, y ella pensó at first she would get up y leave la corte; pero on second thoughts she decided to remain where she was as long as there was room for her.

"I wish you wouldn't squeeze so." Dijo el Dormratón, who was sitting next to her. "I can hardly breathe."

"I can't help it," dijo Alicia muy meekly: "I'm growing."

"You've no right to grow *here*," dijo el Dormratón.

"Don't talk tonterías," dijo Alicia más boldly: "tú sabes que you're growing too."

"Yes, pero I grow at a reasonable pace," dijo el Dormratón: "not in that ridiculous fashion." Y he got up muy sulkily y crossed over al otro lado de la corte.

All this tiempo la Reina had never left off staring al Hatter, y, just as el Dormratón crossed the corte, ella dijo to one of los oficiales de la corte, "Bring me the list of the singers in the last concert!" on which the wretched el Hatter trembled so, que he shook both his shoes off.

"Give your evidence," el Rey repeated angrily, "or I'll have you executed, whether you're nervous or not."

"Soy un pobre hombre, your Majesty," el Hatter began, en una trembling voz, "—y no he comenzado a beber my tea—not above a week or so—y what with the pan-y-mantequilla getting so thin—y the twinkling of the tea—"

"The twinkling of the what?" dijo el Rey.

"It began with the tea," el Hatter replicó.

"Of course twinkling begins with a T!" dijo el Rey sharply. "Do you take me for a dunce? Go on!"

"Soy un pobre hombre," the Hatter went on, "y most cosas twinkled after that—only e; la March Hare dijo—"

"I didn't!" la March Hare interrupió en un gran hurry.

"You did!" dijo el Hatter.

"I deny it!" dijo la March Hare.

"He denies it," dijo el Rey: "leave out that part."

"Bueno, at any rate, el Dormratón dijo—" the Hatter went on, looking anciosamente round to see if he would deny it too: pero el Dormratón negó nada, estando fast dormido.

"Depsués de eso," continuó el Hatter, "I cut some more pan-y-mantequilla—"

"Y qué dijo el Dormratón?" one of el jury preguntó.

"That I can't remembrear," dijo el Hatter.

"You *must* remembrear," remarcó el Rey, "or I'll have you executed."

El miserable Hatter dropped his tea-copa y pan-y-mantequilla, y went down on one knee. "Soy un pobre hombre, su Majestad," he empezó.

"You're una muy pobre speaker," dijo el King.

Here one of the guinea-puercos cheered, y was immediately suppressed by the officers of la corte. (As that is algo de una hard word, I will just explain to you how it was done. They had a large canvas bag, which tied up at the mouth with strings: into this they slipped the guinea-puerco, cabeza first, y then sat upon it.)

"I'm contenta I've seen that done," pensó Alicia. "I've so often read in the newspapers, at the end of trials, 'There was some attempts at applause, which was immediately suppressed by the officers of la corte,' y I never understood what it meant till now."

"If that's all tú sabes about it, you may stand down," continuó el Rey.

"I can't go no lower," dijo el Hatter: "I'm on the floor, as it is."

"Then you may *sit* down," el Rey respondeó.

Here los otros guinea-puercos cheerearon, y was suppressed.

"Come, that finished the guinea-puercos!" pensó Alicia. "Now we shall get on better."

"I'd preferir terminar my tea," dijo el Hatter, with an anciosa mirada a la Reina, who was reading the list of singers.

"You may go," dijo el Rey, y el Hatter hurriedmente left la corte, without even waiting to put his zapatos on.

"—y just take his cabeza off outside," la Reina addeó to one of the officers: pero el Hatter was out of sight before the officer could get a la puerta.

"Call the next witness!" dijo el Rey.

El siguiente witness era la Duquesa's cocinero. She carried the pepper-box en su mano, y Alicia guessed who it was, even before she got into la corte, by the way la gente near la puerta began sneezing all al mismo tiempo.

"Give your evidence," dijo el Rey.

"Sha'n't," dijo el cocinero.

El Rey looked anciosamente at el Rabit Blanco, quien dijo en una low voz, "Your Majesty must cross-examine *this* witness."

"Bueno, if I must, I must," el Rey dijo, with a melancholy air, y, after folding sus brazos y frowneando at el cocinero till sus ojos estaban nearly out of sight, él dijo en una deep voz, "What are tortas made of?"

"Pepper, mostly," dijo el cocinero.

"Treacle," dijo una sleepy voz behind ella.

"Collar that Dormratón," la Reina shriequeó. "Behead at Dormratón! Saquen al Dormratón out of court! Suppresséenlo! Pinchéenlo! Off con sus whiskers!"

Por some minutos the whole corte was en confusión, getting el Dormratón turned out, y, by the tiempo they had settled down otra vez, el cocinero había desaparecido.

"Never mind!" dijo el Rey, with an air of great relief. "Call the next witness." Y he added in an undertono to la Reina, "De veras, my dear, *you* must cross-examine the next witness. It quite makes my forehead ache!"

Alicia watched el Rabit Blanco as he fumbleó over the lista, feeling muy curiosa to see what the next witness would be like, "—for they haven't got mucha evidence *yet*," ella dijo pa'sí misma. Imagine su surprise, cuando el Rabit Blanco read out, en el top de su shrill little vocesita, el nombre "Alicia!"

Capítulo XII

Alicia's Evidencia

"Aquí!" gritó Alicia, quite forgeteando en la flurry del momento how large she had grown en los last few minutos, y ella jumped up in such a hurry that she tipped over la jury-box with the edge of her skirt, upsetting all los jurymen on to las cabezas of the crowd abajo, y there they lay sprawling about, reminding her very mucho of el globe de goldfish she had accidentalmente upset the week before.

"Oh, I *beg* your pardon!" she exclaimed in a tono of great dismay, y began picking them up otra vez as quickly as she could, for the accident of the goldfish kept running in her cabeza, y ella had a vague sort of idea que they must be collected at once y put back into la jury-box, or they would die.

"The trial cannot proceed," dijo el Rey en una muy grave voz, "until all los jurymen are back in their proper places— *all*," he repeated with great emphasis, looking hard at Alicia mientras dijo do.

Alicia looked at la jury-box, y saw que, in her haste, she had put la Lizard in head downwards, y la pobre little cosita estaba waveando its tail about en una melancholy way, estando muy unable pa'moverse. Ella soon got it out otra vez, y put it right; "not that significa mucho," ella dijo pa'sí misma; "I should pensar it would be *quite* as mucho use in the trial one way up as the other."

As soon as el jury had un poquito recovered from the shock of being upset, y their slates y pencils had been found y handed back to them, they set to work muy diligently to write out a history of the accident, all except la Lizard, who seemed too mucho overcome to do cualquier cosa pero sit with its mouth open, gazing up into the roof of la corte.

"What do you know about this business?" el Rey dijo a Alicia.

"Nada," dijo Alicia.

"Nada *whatever?*" persistió el Rey.

"Nada whatever," dijo Alicia.

"That's very important," el Rey dijo, turning to el jury. They were just beginning to write this down on their slates, when el Rabit Blanco interrupted: "*Un*important, your Majesty means, of course," él dijo en un muy respectful tono, pero frowneando y making caras at him mientras él spokeaba.

"*Un*importante, of course, I meant," el Rey hastily dijo, y went on to himself in an undertono, "important— unimportant—unimportant—important—" as if he were trying which word sounded best.

Algunos of el jury wrote it down "important", y some "unimportant". Alicia could see this, as she was near enough to look over their slates; "pero it doesn't matter a bit," she pensó pa'sí misma.

At this momento el Rey, who had been for some tiempo busily writing in his note-book, cackled out "Silence!" y read out from his book, "Regla Forty-two. *All personas más que una mile altas to leave la corte.*"

Everybody miró at Alicia.

"*I'm* not a mile alta," dijo Alicia.

"You are," dijo el Rey.

"Nearly dos miles alta," agregó la Reina.

"Bueno, I sha'n't ir, en cualquier rate," dijo Alicia: "besides, that's not una regular regla: you invented it just ahora."

"It's the oldest regla en el libro," dijo el Rey.

"Then it ought to be Número Uno," dijo Alicia.

El Rey se turneó pale, y shut his note-book hastily. "Consider your verdict," él dijo to el jury, en una low, trembleante voz.

"Hay más evidencia to come yet, por favor su Majesty," dijo el Rabit Blanco, jumping up in a great hurry; "this paper has just been picked up."

"What's in it?" dijo la Reina.

"I haven't opened it todavía," dijo el Rabit Blanco, "pero it seems to be una carta, written by the prisoner to—to somebody."

"It must have been that," dijo el Rey, "unless it was written to nobody, which isn't usual, tú sabes."

"Who is it directed to?" dijo uno de los jurymen.

"It isn't directed at all," dijo el Rabit Blanco; "in facto, there's nada written on the *outside*." He unfolded the paper as he spoke, y added "It isn't una carta, after all: it's a set of verses."

"Are they in the prisoner's handwriting?" asked another de los jurymen.

"No, they're not," dijo el Rabit Blanco, "y that's la cosa más extraña about it." (El jury all looked puzzleado.)

"He must have imitated somebody else's hand," dijo el Rey. (El jury all brightened up otra vez.)

"Por favor su Majesty," dijo el Knave, "I didn't write it, y they can't prove I did: there's no name signed at the end."

"If you didn't sign it," dijo el Rey, "that only makes the matter worse. You *must* have meant some mischief, or else you'd have signed your name like an honest man."

Hubo un general clapping de manos at this: it was la primera de veras clever cosa que el Rey había dicho ese día.

"That *proves* his guilt," dijo la Reina. "so, off con—"

"It proves nada of the sort!" dijo Alicia. "Why, you don't even know what they're about!"

"Léelas," dijo el Rey.

El Rabit Blanco put on sus gafas. "Where shall I begin, por favor su Majesty?" he asked.

"Begin at the beginning," el Rey dijo gravemente, "y go on till you come to the end: then stop."

Hubo un silencio muerto en la corte, whilst el Rabit Blanco read out estos versos:—

"Me dijeron you had been to her,
Y mentioned me to him:
Ella me dio un good caracter,
Pero dijo I could not swim.

Él les mandó palabra I had not gone
(Sabemos it to be true):
Si ella should push el matter on,
Qué would become of you?

I gave her one, they gave him two,
You gave us tres o more;
They all returned de él to you,
Aunque they were mine before.

Si yo or she should chance to be
Envueltos en este affair,
Él trusts a ti pa'set them free,
Exacto as we were.

My noción was que you had been
(Before she had this fit)
Un obstacle que came between
Him, y ourselves, and it.

Don't let him saber she liked them best,
Pues this must ever be
Un secret, kept from all the rest,
Entre yourself and me."

"That's the most important pieza of evidence we've heard todavía," dijo el Rey, rubbeando sus manos; "so now let el jury—"

"If any one of them can explain it," dijo Alicia, (she had grown so large en los last few minutos que she wasn't a bit afraid of interrupting him,) "I'll give him sixpence. *I* don't believe there's an atom of meaning in it."

El jury all wrote down on their slates, "*She* doesn't believe there's an atom of meaning in it," pero none of them attempted to explain the paper.

"If there's no meaning in it," dijo el Rey, "que saves a world of trouble, tú sabes, as we needn't try to find any. And yet I don't know," he went on, spreading out the verses on his knee, y looking at them con un ojo; "I seem to see some meaning in them, after all. '—*Dije I could not swimmear*—' you can't swim, can you?" he added, turning to el Knave.

El Knave shook his cabeza sadly. "Do I look like it?" él

dijo. (Which he certainly did *not*, being made entirely of cardboard.)

"All right, so far," dijo el Rey, y he went on muttering over the verses to himself: "'*Sabemos it to be true*'—that's el jury, of course—'*Si ella should push el matter on*'—that must be la Reina—'Qué would become de ti?'—Qué, indeed!—'Yo le di a ella one, they gave him dos—' why, that must be what he did con las tortas, tú sabes—"

"Pero, it goes on '*They all returned from him to you*,'" dijo Alicia.

"Why, there they are!" dijo el Rey triumphantemente, pointing a las tortas en la mesa. "Nada can be clearer than *that*. Then otra vez—'*Before she had this fit*—' you never had fits, my dear, yo pienso?" él dijo a la Reina.

"Nunca!" dijo la Reina furiousamente, throwing an inkstand at the Lizard as she spoke. (The unfortunate mini Bill had left off writing on his slate con un dedo, as he found it made no mark; pero he now hastily began otra vez, using el ink, que was trickling down su cara, as long as it lasted.)

"Then the words don't *fit* you," dijo el Rey, looking round la corte con una sonrisa. There was a dead silence.

"It's a pun!" el Rey agregó in an offended tono, y everybody laughed, "Let el jury consider su verdicto," el Rey dijo, for about el twentieth tiempo ese día.

"No, no!" dijo la Reina. "Sentence primero—verdicto después."

"Stuff y tonterías!" dijo Alicia loudeamente. "The idea of having the sentence first!"

"Hold your lengua!" dijo la Reina, turning púrpura.

"I wo'n't!" dijo Alicia.

"Off con su cabeza!" la Reina shouteó at the top of her voz. Nobody moved.

"Who cares for you?" dijo Alicia, (she had grown to her full size by this tiempo.) "You're nada pero un pack de cartas!"

At this the whole pack rose up into the air, y came flying down upon her: she gave un pequeño scream, half of fright y half of anger, y tried to beat them off, y found herself lying on the bank, con su cabeza in el lap of her hermana, who was gently brushing away some dead leaves that had fluttered down from los árboles upon su cara.

"Despiértate, Alicia dear!" dijo su hermana; "Why, what a long sleep you've had!"

"Oh, I've had such a curious sueño!" dijo Alicia, y ella told her hermana, tan bien como ella could remembrearlas, todas las extrañas Adventuras of hers que you have just been reading about; y when she had finished, su hermana kissed her, y dijo, "It *was* a curious sueño, dear, certainly: pero now run in to your tea; it's getting late." So Alicia got up y ran off, pensando while she ran, tan bien como ella might, what a wonderful sueño it had been.

Pero su hermana sat still solo as she left her, leaning su cabeza en su mano, watching the setting sun, y pensando de la pequeña Alicia y todas sus wonderful Adventures, till she too began dreaming after a fashion, y este era su sueño:—

First, she dreamed de la pequeña Alicia herself, y once otra vez las tiny manos were clasped upon her knee, y the bright eager ojos were looking up a los suyos—she could hear the very tonos de su voz, y see that extraña little toss of her cabeza to keep back the wandering pelo that *would* always get into her ojos—y still as she listened, or seemed to listen, the whole lugar around her became alive con las extrañas creaturas de su pequeña hermanita's sueño.

El long pasto rustled a sus pies as el Rabit Blanco hurried by—el frightened Ratón splashed his way a través de la neighbouring pool—she could oir el rattle de las tea-copas mientras la March Hare y sus friends compartían su never-ending meal, y the shrill voz la Reina ordenó her unfortunate guests to execución—otra vez the pig-baby was sneezing on la Duquesa's knee, while plates y platos crashed around it— otra vez el shriek del Gryfón, el squeaking de la Lizard's slate-pencil, y el choking de los suppressed guinea-puercos, fillearon el aire, mixed up con los distantes sobs of la miserable Mock Tortuga.

So ella siguió sentada, con los ojos cerrados, y half believed herself en Wonderlandia, though ella sabía she had pero to

open them otra vez, y all would cambiar to dull la realidad—
el pasto would be only rustling en el viento, y la pool
rippleando to the waving de los reeds—las rattling tea-copas
would cambiar to tinkling sheep-bells, y la Reina's shrill cries
a la voz del shepherd boy—y the sneeze del baby, el shriek del
Gryfón, y all thy otros ruidos extraños, would cambiar (ella
sabía) to the confused clamour of the busy farm-yard—while
the lowing of the cattle in the distance would take the place
of la Mock Tortuga's heavy sobs.

Finalmente, ella pictureó pa'sí misma cómo esta misma
little hermanita of hers would, in the after-time, be herself a
grown woman; y how she would keep, through all her riper
years, the simple y loving corazón de su childhood: y y cómo
would gather about los otros little niñitos, y make *their* ojos
brillantes y eager with many a cuento extraño, perhaps even
con el sueño of Wonderlandia de hace mucho tiempo: y cómo
ella would feel con todas their simple sorrows, y find un
placer en todos sus simple joys, remembreando her own
child-vida, y los happy summer días.